YOU ARE NOT ALONE

ALONE

DON'T GIVE UP

by

Linda LS Larson

Cover Design by Serena Daphn

Author's Photograph by Greg Crowder

ACKNOWLEDGEMENT

Special thanks to Brittany S. McKinley for her excellent editing skills, and for being such a joy to work with.

DEDICATION

This book is dedicated to my son, Timothy, and my sister, Diane. Thank you for your love, devotion, and kind hearts. You are the lights of my life. I love you dearly.

Table of Contents

Introduction

I have always felt that God has been watching over us all. I've made a lot of mistakes, but the older I get, the more I seem to feel that our lives are on important journeys for our souls. I have had some visions, met inspiring people, and sensed moments that God was reminding me of his being beside me. I have pulled back so many times from giving up. I believe that God, his angels, and the belief in an afterlife, be it in heaven or reincarnation, have given me hope and courage.

I have laughed and cried. Now I'm reflecting on all the thoughts, emotional trials, successes, failures, lessons learned, and wondrous special moments that have colored my journey.

I hope my words in this book will inspire, assist, and comfort you on your path. I yearn for and encourage you to enjoy your life. You are loved and never alone.

Legal Notes/Disclaimer

Chapter 1. Childhood

Some, many, or perhaps just a few of us may have had events that brought the supernatural into our lives. Were we afraid? You may have been, or maybe not.

My experiences were not really threatening but often were totally surprising to me. One happened when I was just a little girl. I don't even remember how old I was. Was I five or seven? I only remember what happened; that I will never forget.

I awoke suddenly one night. I felt someone or something was looking at me and very closely. My eyes sprang open and I stared with surprise at the soft dark eyes of a man with long flowing black hair. His expression was kind. He seemed to be studying me thoughtfully. I remember staring at him. I knew it was a him. I wasn't fearful. I asked him quietly, "Who are you?"

He seemed to pull back and tilt his head. Did he know me or not? He seemed almost pleased. I don't know what about him made me think that. Was it a feeling of happiness or kindness? My young mind was in awe. Suddenly he seemed to float around the bed as he looked at me. He had no body, just a head with hair that sparkled and drifted softly in the air. His face began to glow with light. He said nothing. The silence built between us until I couldn't help but blurt out a call for my mother. I wanted her to see him.

"Mama, Mama!" my words tumbled out. Suddenly my fascinating visitor dissipated along with his light.

My door sprang open, and Mama rushed into the room. "What's wrong?" She sounded worried. I jumped up. "Did you see him? Who is he? There was a man in here." I was more excited than alarmed. I also should have said, "What was it?" But he wasn't frightening. Mama looked around my room with a grumble and said, "No one is here. Go to sleep. You'll wake everyone up." Then she moved quickly to her room. I guess she sensed I wasn't afraid. She never mentioned it in the morning. I think she felt I was dreaming.

I knew that it was real, and though I'll always remember him, I never saw him again.

Who or what was he? Was he an angel? I'm sure I'm not so special that I deserved a visit from Jesus, God's own son. But I'd like to think that he was sent by God and not some alien race. I usually didn't wake up during the night when I was a child. I never dreamed of anything like him. Actually, I don't remember my childhood dreams. I'd like to think now that the incident was my first meeting with my guardian angel. Why not come to that conclusion? It is comforting and harmless. In fact, I was delighted by the experience. Whatever he was, he meant me no harm, of that I was sure. If there are beings from other galaxies or dimensions watching us or angels sent by God, I do not feel that I will be harmed by them.

It actually made me feel wonderful about God and the universe. I think we are being watched by Him and/or other kindly beings. I don't believe that they always do what we want them to do, like cure our pain or save our lives, but they do walk beside us.

I remember once going to a psychic fair and having someone give me a reading. I know some of you are passionate about going to these fairs for fun and in earnest, and there are many who may think I'm nuts or silly. But I loved the experience. I'm not sure that I believed the woman that I talked to, but I liked her. I later saw many psychics that I thought were phonies, but this one stood out positively for me. She said that I had two guardian angels. She called one—Carl. I laughed because I couldn't imagine a guardian angel having such a common and simple name. I have forgotten the other name. But as the years went by, I have always sensed one angel with me. Could she be right or just a lady eager to make an easy profit? I hope she was correct in her message.

Have I convinced myself that angels are real because I like the idea? I don't think so. I sometimes feel a presence. Could it be one angel or more watching over me and giving me solace? Was it my childhood night visitor? Sometimes I just feel a sweet type of silence.

But those special times are when he or something intervenes in my life. Of course, I always hope for a savior from my troubles, but I usually have to desperately figure my own way out of them. However, there are times, when I sense the nearness of God and his angels. This happens when I've quieted my thoughts and resigned my thinking and body to silence. It's usually after I've gone through stress and have given myself over to needing help and feeling that I can't do something alone. I'd be worried and tense, but then my body totally gives in to relaxation. That's when a solution seems to pop before me visually or in my mind, and I'm ready to listen.

You too may have had these experiences. You also may have figured this out from your childhood. We all need to listen. Then we can feel and hear God, or His emissaries. Don't be afraid. Evil is in mankind, not God. Maybe a solution to our every problem doesn't come as fast as we would like, but it happens eventually. We might prefer a different solution but it will get solved.

I'm not afraid of God and the universe, only people who are sick mentally, those who make hurtful decisions for themselves and in turn affect others. If we can help them, that is good. If you feel unsafe and unable to deal with them, leave them to others who are more capable and even trained for such a task. Or as a last resort, pass it over to God Himself. Everyone has their own path in life, but we must try to never hurt others intentionally.

Is there order to the universe and God's work? I think order can be seen all over, when we quiet our minds and look around. I especially notice that time seems to go so much more slowly in childhood. We see things more vividly. Those memories stick much harder onto our minds. Maybe it's because we are young, forming, and need more time and depth to process the events taking place around us. Our environment and family during our childhoods have such a deep impact on our souls' growth and happiness.

I think that God is especially close to us during our youth. If we are hurt, is it an accident or designed by our souls, maybe even by God?

We may never know for sure when we are alive. But possibly our souls learn from it. Perhaps there are reasons. I hope so.

Some people seem to have life so much easier than others, but maybe it all evens out in the end of our souls' journeys. I hope there is fairness, if not in this life, then in another. I think it may be true.

I also know there was a feeling of warmth and safety when I experienced my childhood contact with a spirit, and I've felt it many times since. We do not need to be afraid.

If nature makes order, even from what we perceive as chaos, so go humans. It makes living interesting, although sometimes scary and frustrating.

Our childhood journeys are important beginnings for us all.

Chapter 2. Nighttime

The older we become, the more we miss family members that have died. We hurt so badly over their loss.

Once I felt very sad when I crawled into bed. I had wallowed in depression from extreme loss and loneliness over the death of my twin brother, my younger brother, and my mother and father. I'm sure most of us have had death come back to haunt us, stabbing us with those intense feelings of missing our deceased relatives.

Suddenly in the middle of the night, I jerked awake. I felt a presence. I don't know if it was a vivid dream or not, but it felt real. I saw people kneeling beside my bed, along the sides and at the foot. One lady wore a frontier bonnet and white apron. Men in suits were interspersed between the women. They did not look up, just bowed their heads and moved their lips silently.

Stunned, I blurted out in staccato, "What are you doing? Who are you? Why are you here? What do you want? Are you praying? For me?"

Now I was very frightened. No one answered.

"Get out of here!" I shouted. "Go away. You're scaring me." I was trembling and confused. "Please go away."

These strange visitors raised their heads slowly, stared at me gravely, and vanished.

They were gone. My heart was still pounding. My eyelids suddenly felt heavy, and I closed my eyes. The beating of my heart slowed to a quiet pace. I sank back into a peaceful sleep.

The next morning, I awoke refreshed. I stretched happily and then suddenly remembered. I looked around tentatively, but the night visitors were gone.

I carefully flipped back my covers and stepped onto the soft carpet. I took another step and almost stumbled as I felt a hard object beneath my bare foot. I looked down curiously and wondered what I had knocked over and stepped upon.

I reached down and slowly picked up the object, turning it over in my hand. I suddenly felt shocked. In my hand was one of my brother's medals from the Vietnam War. It was his purple heart.

My twin brother, Tom, had died many years before. My family had given his medals to me so as to save and treasure. They had been secured in a box at the bottom of my drawer. It had been many years since I had taken them out. I now lived alone in my house. My son had moved out some time ago and was happily living his own life. I was the only one here. How did the medal end up on the floor?

Suddenly I realized, awestruck at what I thought had happened. I believe it to this very day. My brother had been in my room and pulled out the medal. I felt he had come back to help me overcome my sorrow at missing him and my parents so terribly. I had felt so very alone and depressed. Was he telling me to stay encouraged? Was he saying that I was not alone and that he would always be with me? Was he saying that my ancestors and he were praying for me? I'd like to think all of the above. I now felt the warm flood of relief and peace.

I am breathless now as I remember that night and morning. I am convinced that it was not just a dream from my imagination, but that God and the people in the afterlife care about the living. They continually try to help us through their prayers. I believe that they watch over us in another plane of existence. They are still alive, and we remain connected. When the pain of feeling totally alone comes, we can remember our loved ones and hang on to life.

I felt comforted. There are those who would deny this, I realize that. But I treasure that I was shown a window into my soul's journey, and I am not alone.

You should also go ahead in peace. Smile and be happy. Your loved ones are there for you too. You are not on your own.

When we touch something that our deceased family and friends handled, or look at their pictures, we bring them close. We might also be attending an event that reminds us of them. I think this means they are near. We just need to calm our busy minds and feel the peace they bring to us.

At another time, I was stunned by a tragic incident that involved a dear friend. Her fifteen-year-old daughter had committed suicide. It was shattering for her family.

On the night before the funeral, I awoke suddenly and saw the young girl with a bright smile on her face. Her normally straight hair was now in lovely curls. She sat within a soft light on the edge of a dresser near my bed. She said, "Don't worry. I'm okay. I'm good." She grinned and vanished.

The next day, I told her mother. She thanked me and seemed to believe my vision. She had been afraid that her beautiful, sweet, gentle daughter would be kept out of heaven because of her suicide. I think we both know now that she was living in the afterlife as a happy child of God.

Whether my vision was just a dream and not a divine connection, I could never say for sure. But—I sincerely think that the message was correct and sent for a reason. That loving child would always be treasured by God. God believes in eternal love and mankind, despite our many mistakes.

Nighttime can refresh our bodies. It can also bring dreams, memories, healing, and glimpses into the afterlife, which can give us hope and reassurance that our lives are important. We are valuable. We are loved.

Chapter 3. Lost

Have you been lost? Most of us have experienced being physically lost once or even many times. How did you find your way again?

I eventually found my way each time but often never as planned. When you find your way, it can be after extreme frustration and feelings of hopelessness.

Once I had come to Sacramento, California for a play audition. I am sometimes an actress, and often a very determined one. I had been visiting relatives in a town nearby and had never been to Sacramento before. So, I was off on my adventure.

I arrived and searched for parking. I soon traveled some distance away from the audition building. Where would I park? Suddenly I spotted a place. Delighted, I pulled up where there were no meters but rather poles with numbers. A man was climbing out of his car next to me. He was friendly, and we chatted briefly. I noted my pole was marked with the number three. I looked around, thinking I had memorized my spot with landmarks. Plus, my location had a number. I felt reassured and walked off. My mind reviewed the words to my audition material. I repeated my speeches over and over as I walked. I was totally submerged in my dramatic piece. I suddenly looked up and saw the building in which I was to perform.

Later I emerged happily from that building: all had gone well! I scurried towards my car. I felt giddy and confident. Suddenly after many blocks, I came to a stop. Where was I? Where is my car? I began to question if I had taken a wrong turn. No, there was a three on the pole in front of me, but no car.

I walked a few blocks back and set off in the other direction, again I reached a three on a pole but no car. I tried again, over and over again. I kept changing directions and searching. It was a very hot day, and soon I was dripping with perspiration and exhausted. I couldn't find my old faithful automobile. It seemed invisible. I saw a postman and asked him why there were so many parking places with the number three on the poles. "Is there a pattern?" I inquired; he didn't know. Discouraged, I thought maybe that I could ask a policeman to drive me around, but I realized he probably wouldn't do it. I felt like I wanted to cry, and I was so awfully tired now.

I spotted a grassy area ahead with a bench. I plopped down. Mopping my sweaty face, I tried to calm myself. I was feeling extreme anxiety and hopelessness. How could I be so stupid as to get lost?

Time seemed to hold still. A gentle breeze began to dry my body. I was no longer frantic, just exhausted. I sat quietly, and then slowly I was drawn to gaze to my right. There stood a stone statue in the form of a graceful woman with arms embracing a small child. I thought: "Such beautiful love for that child!" I felt a sudden rush of comprehension: I was the small child being embraced by God, or possibly the Virgin Mary. To me it was saying, "Don't be afraid. I love you, and I'm here for you." I was overcome with joy as tears rolled down my face.

Suddenly, I felt the need to turn to my left and look. There before me was my car, parked on the street beside a post that said the number three. It was only a few feet away. I had never noticed the park or the statue before. I had been obsessed with the number on the pole.

I climbed into my car. I was overwhelmed with relief, from not just finding it but feeling such an emotional impact of having been hugged by the arms of God. My hands began to shake as I put them on the steering wheel. "He loves me. ME!"

God loves YOU too. We must *never* forget it. I think He lets us try on our own, but when we are lost and stop struggling, He reaches out and touches our minds. Our thoughts clear, and we can go forward with a wondrous feeling of being noticed and loved.

Years later, I was lost in another city, none other than beautiful San Francisco. I know what you're thinking: "Again?" Oh yes, again. It was during a dark night, however. I had been driving to my aunt's house and had come along a different route than the one I usually traveled. I was lost in the hills for hours. 1:00 PM, 2:00 PM, 3 PM, 4. I ended up going on different freeways and went down the west side of the coast and then later on the bay side. I felt foolish and terribly alone.

Frantic and exhausted, I finally pulled over and closed my eyes in hopelessness. I didn't know what to do. I cried out loudly to myself and then to the universe. "God, I'm so lost. Would you help me?"

Suddenly my thoughts grew still. I breathed deeply and quietly. I slowly looked up and gasped. There on a sign in front of me was a street name that I recognized. I knew where I was! I was no longer lost. I couldn't believe it at first. It was right there.

That small moment in my life became a happy memory of God's answering even my little prayers. I had felt very alone in my car in the dark streets, and suddenly the hopelessness was gone. I had this feeling of awe that still lingers with me even thirty years later.

I also think often of another spiritual intervention in which ordinary people did special acts of human kindness along with a wonderful "human angel." Or was he a heavenly angel? I don't know.

I was in my twenties. My son's father and I had broken up our relationship when my son was still an infant. I was working as a waitress in the evenings and at night, and always came home to my apartment building very late. I had picked up my son first and paid the sitter, my left-over tips and baby bottles still in my big diaper bag. With my keys in hand, I started up the steps to the door at the building's main entrance.

Suddenly a man in a mask sprang from the shadows behind me. He yanked me around and shoved a gun up to my face, as I clutched my baby.

It's strange how a person acts when they are in danger. Let's just say that I reacted in a manner that was not helpful to me or perhaps I could more accurately say, a *stupid* manner! That is to say, I made a huge mistake. You see, I started laughing at him! It was because of the man's mask; it looked like a cowboy bandana, and he seemed like a ridiculous cowboy. I couldn't help giggling.

Of course, the guy got angry. He grabbed my keys roughly and yanked away the diaper bag, before shoving me back against the door. Realizing my mistake, I apologized and asked nervously if he would please not take my keys and the bag. I said that it had all my baby bottles and food. I grabbed at the bag, but he jerked it roughly away. "NO!" he hissed, and then turned, plunging into the darkness of the streets.

My son and I were alive and that was good. But as I stood there holding my very small sleeping child, I suddenly realized the gravity of what had just happened. I had been robbed at gunpoint! What if he came back?

The thought hit me hard. I'm alone with my baby, the door to the building is locked, and it's very dark outside. I started shaking. I pushed the buzzer for the apartment manager. I told him who I was and that I was holding my baby. I said that I had been robbed and that the man had taken my keys. I asked if he could open the door for us.

"Leave me alone. I don't care," the manager retorted. The intercom clicked off. I slowly sat down on the steps and held my child close to my heart. I just stared out into the night feeling empty, lost, and alone.

Suddenly a man staggered out of the shadows and came towards me. My breath caught in my throat. I was frightened again. I think the man was drunk. Was he going to be kind or mean to me? What was I going to do? I stood up slowly, gasping for air.

"You okay, Lady?" the man asked. His hands shook as he approached the door, took out his key and turned it in the lock. He pulled the handle and held the door open for me to enter. I started sobbing as we walked in. He gently eased me down into a chair. I babbled hysterically about what the manager had said and that a robber had taken my keys, my baby's food and bottles, as well as my waitress tips.

I suddenly realized that I wouldn't be able to get into my apartment either, and that thought only made me feel worse. I couldn't stop the tears as I clutched my sleeping son. My baby looked so innocent and unaware of his mother's despair. Through all this, my drunk friend listened with kindness. Finally, I calmed down.

People started coming into the lobby. They called the police. Unbelievably, the manager still would not open his apartment door, even for the police, so they just let it go.

But that manager! The man had always dressed in fancy suits and had treated me respectfully, which had led me to believe that he was a good person. I couldn't understand why he was not helping me. I realized that people aren't always what they appear to be.

On the other hand, the tenants in the building were all low income, and yet they took the time to be very kind and giving. They banded together to try to get me back into my apartment. They couldn't open the door at first. I was living on the ninth floor at the time. Finally, two men decided to crawl onto the fire escape and over towards a ledge. They struggled but finally managed to cross the ledge and open the window to my apartment. Climbing through, they were able to open my apartment door from within. It was all quite a dangerous feat. I was overwhelmed by the kindness and dedication these people showed towards helping me. All during the action, my drunk "friend" stood quietly beside me.

Finally, the worst was over. I collapsed into the refuge of my apartment. My child and I had survived the night.

Early the next morning, I heard a knock on my door. It was my "savior" from the night before, and he was no longer drunk. Without a word, this sweet caring man, who I had feared at the beginning, then handed me a large paper bag before racing away down the corridor. "Thank you, Sir," I shouted, stumbling over my words in surprise. He disappeared around the corner.

I stared in awe at the bag and slowly closed the door. I sat at the table and started looking through the contents. It was heaped with food, and at the bottom of the bag there rested a five-dollar bill. It was an amazing moment for me. I was stunned by his kindness, and I still am.

I never saw the man again. I asked people about him. No one knew him or where he lived in the building. I can't help but believe that he was my angel. Whether he was a human angel or heavenly one, I felt blessed by him and the others in the building.

I'm convinced that people and angels are often God's emissaries on Earth. They will come through for us when we are in need. So instead of it all being one huge horrible experience, it now stays in my mind as a very special and wonderful memory of when humanity, and possibly God again, touched my life in a beautiful way.

I realize that not every difficult or truly awful event in our lives will end positively, but there are enough if we take the time to reflect. We need to look back in order to appreciate that there is goodness in many men and women all over the world, and that there is a God. We are not lost to the eternal whims of the universe. God knows what we are going through. He is beside us. We are not walking alone through time.

Chapter 4. Stress

Stress is constantly influencing our happiness. God knows the day-to-day pressures we are under at times and the effects of stress on your life and mine. We all experience it, so we must consider and handle it. Everything I say to you, I say to myself and do so many times. I *need* to hear it, just as you might.

You are not alone in dealing with stress. Please don't let it overwhelm you, and try your best not to fear it. We want to find positive solutions, even though it can be difficult.

Oddly enough, stress can save your life when you need to run or fight back, but it can also hurt you at other times if you do nothing about it. Usually it is best to act. Don't be afraid to do so. If you need a bigger plan rather than a quick solution, go for it. Sometimes your first decision is the correct one and leads to the best ending. If it doesn't go the way you hoped, at least you tried, and that's all we can really expect anyone to do. Be proud that you put forth your best effort. If it doesn't work, try again. Don't get discouraged! Eventually you'll kick that stress to the curb. And—if you can do it once, you can do it again.

If you are terribly worried, talk to someone, get those words out of the cage of your mind and into the light. The situation might look less threatening then and show forth more solutions. Your mind will feel lighter by sharing your feelings, and you can then think more clearly about how to go forward. Even if you don't take your friend's advice, you can listen and evaluate. Deep down, you may already know the answer to the problem you're facing.

Stress can harm your body physically, so do deal with it. Don't hide the fact that it's affecting you. It only gets heavier, more confusing, and more complicated, if you *don't* face it. I am not saying that we must be brave at all times. Goodness, I don't always feel brave. So don't be hard on yourself; if you choose to run and hide, it may be the right choice at the time. Just do your best. You *can* move forward.

You are a special person with wonderful qualities. Speak to yourself with praise. You may not believe it, but you are absolutely fantastic! There is no one else like you. Give yourself this compliment over and over again. Repeat to yourself that you are talented, attractive, kind, courageous, smart, and unique. You are made in God's likeness, and His creation has no mistakes. Everything has a purpose to God. Men and women make mistakes when they detour to the dark side because of the existence of free will. But, when it comes to giving life, God doesn't make mistakes.

Put on your gorgeous smile and face the world. Wiggle and strut, and shove that stress off. Imagine it is lifting away and disintegrating. Practice creating that feeling, and picture it in your mind. You are floating off down a road with no bondage or stress. You are going to feel so much better when you drop all your worrying, and you will stop its adverse effects on your body and mind.

Quick decisions can be best, especially when in danger. My son once said that he'd been confronted on a dark street when he was walking to his car. A gang of five guys seemed to come out of nowhere, and they bluntly told him that they wanted to beat him up. My son didn't know these people. He is a quiet, non- violent guy by nature, and no one had ever threatened him like this before. He was also in a fairly calm neighborhood, so he was shocked by this occurrence.

Now my son is very strong and works out all the time, but he looked at that hostile group and felt outnumbered. He made a quick and ultimately right decision to bolt to the nearest house and start turning the door knob; he shouted, "Hey, Dad, it's me!" The guys took off. Whew! He was relieved. Me too!

Sometimes you must run in a different direction mentally or physically, when you feel something is wrong or that you will be hurt. My son was in stress from a dangerous situation, and he made the correct choice. Fighting, arguing, surrendering, or offering money were other options that he could have chosen. But his decision was fast, and it worked for him.

For whatever situation you find yourself in, you too may need to run a different way: that could yank off your stress and heartache. Or, maybe you need to end a relationship with your partner or friend. Both of you can then pull free and go forward, unburdened by a former decision that didn't work out. You can always change your mind—it's up to you. You do have possibilities in your choices. You need to be happy. Don't stay in your choices, if they are bringing you that anchor of stress. You must free yourself from unhappy situations.

There may be times when it's too late to make corrections. We may wish with all our hearts that we could change things, but we can't. So instead… charge ahead. Advance as best you can. Move with courage and try to be positive.

Also, remember to seek out professional help when stress becomes too rough for you to handle alone or you can no longer think clearly. I am giving advice and presenting ideas from my experiences and thoughts; use them only if you see them as good choices. I am not a professional health worker. My opinions may not be like yours, and I could be wrong. Goodness, I've made enough mistakes to know that. Also, professionals may be better sources of guidance. Do consider them if you are in serious distress. It is up to you to choose what option is best for you.

God is with you. Treasure and protect yourself. Be kind to others and to yourself. God wants you to be happy and succeed in life. He does not want you to be blinded by stress. Clear away the shadows of fear in your mind. Step up. Be proud of you. You *can* move ahead. With effort, you'll be standing tall and walking with confidence, because you have freed yourself from thoughts and situations that were crippling you. You did it! It feels good, doesn't it? And you did it.

Chapter 5. Quitting

When you believe that you are coping, but repeated failures clobber your confidence, and you feel like giving up on life, *don't*. Please don't.

I totally understand. I have felt such heavy depression also. If you possess guns, please give them to someone else to hold for you, or, if need be, just sell them. We don't always make good decisions when our emotions are concerned. If you did something drastic to yourself, your soul would despair greatly. You would also hurt your family and friends terribly. They *will* move on with their lives as best they can, but yours will be gone from this Earth. You may live again in the hereafter, but there would be no turning back or returning to this life.

Seek out your family and friends if you feel you are a danger to yourself, they might be able to help. Seek out a teacher or the minister of a church. But if the depression is very serious and no one seems to be able to help you, seek out a professional for help. Call the suicide help line, listen to their advice. If one pro doesn't work for you the way you need them to, keep looking. You'll find the right person! Time passes and you'll feel differently as it goes by. In the end, you'll be happy that you chose to continue your life.

Don't go through heavy depression alone. You are valuable and deserve help. Depression can block your ability to make good decisions. God wants you to live a good life. You can do this. He gave you your life. You are precious to Him. Don't ever give up.

Don't let nasty selfish people drive you to call it quits. Don't argue with them, get away from them! They are toxic and hurt everyone they touch. Just walk away.

I'm sure we have all been totally discouraged by failure or perceived failures. Sometimes it feels that it happens too often. In some instances, the failures keep tumbling down upon us until it feels like we're beneath a monstrous pile of disappointments. They seem to be chopping our self-confidence to pieces, and all we want to do is cry. I too have felt that way.

Let's turn to our dreams now and our plans for our lives. Reflect on yours, just as I do on mine, and learn. I had a dream goal, and I wanted to pursue it. It may have seemed trivial to some, but it was my dream. I loved acting in plays and film; but for the last few years I had not landed even a small job. I recently moved to New York for a period and failed to get anywhere job wise, despite having gone to many auditions. Believe me, I know the statistics for success in acting. I also know there are less roles for women, especially at my present age, but I thought if I tried hard enough, I could find work.

I couldn't afford an apartment in metropolitan New York City. Therefore, I was living in a basement of a home in a New York suburb. I dragged myself up and down hills for miles to the commuter train depot in order to meet my daily ride to the city. I did this every day. I carried my music, pictures, resumes, change of clothes and shoes, my umbrella, my jacket, my purse, and my lunch in my stuffed bag. I would arrive at the train exhausted and often dripping from the heat or rain. My outfit was wrinkled and my hair a mess. Once in NYC, I pounded the pavement from audition to audition. I did the same journey back daily, many times at midnight from my auditions and classes. At night, once home, I would flop onto my air mattress and was either very cold or very hot *and* uncomfortable since the thermostat was locked up by the owner. I was all on my own. I was worried about money, tired, alone and often discouraged. I was feeling really old. My dream of New York acting work was not coming true, even though I had tried so very hard. This time, I gave up. I couldn't do it alone anymore. I needed a change. Sometimes you feel deep in your soul that an approach is not working. This was one of those times.

Finally, I moved away, returning to a small town outside of Los Angeles, where I have lived for many years. Even here I proceeded to fail repeatedly. I thought my change would revitalize me, but this time I had trouble. My failure in New York had battered my confidence. At one audition, I needed to dance for the part as well as act and sing. I'm older now and am not a pro dancer. I thought I might be considered anyway—I was wrong. I danced badly, my confidence was gone, and I was devastated. My whole body was trembling so much that I couldn't sing my song with commitment. I heard this strange light shaky voice coming out of me. I was cut off after only a couple of bars of my song. As you might expect, I didn't get the job. The tears came when I reached my car. I felt awful. I had disappointed myself severely.

I began to isolate myself from people, and I crawled into my hole of depression. I never wanted to come out, not ever again. I had tried so very hard to succeed, yet felt totally overwhelmed and defeated. I was "swimming" in a deep black hole. I was losing my will. I didn't want to see friends anymore. I didn't want to go out of my apartment. I knew how heavily depressed I was. I also knew how dangerous it was for me to stay this way.

So, I had a hard talk with myself and chose a crazy solution. Why not, if it helped and it did. I needed love badly but was resisting getting it from people. So, ready for this? I got a dog from the pound. I know you are chuckling; me too! That adorable creature was just what I needed at the moment. She gave me unconditional love, and I began to feel the discouragement lift. I had wanted to quit on life. I had felt old and unwanted. I had yearned to just curl up and disappear. Now that need was gone. The pressure on my chest evaporated. I wasn't alone. I had needed someone or something to pull me up. I could have chosen people. *You* can choose people. My cute little dog did this for me. If this hadn't worked, I would have turned to a professional.

I also started to reread the first sections of my book here. I decided that I should follow my own advice. I needed to pull myself back and be more objective. The world and I won't come to an end just because I didn't get some jobs. I still had a family and friends that cared about me. I had to stop looking at the negatives and start looking at the positives in myself and in my life. I had forgotten how important this was, and truthfully, we all need to do this. Depression can close off the practical wisdom of our minds, and we need to kick open the door to let in the fresh air and look at our situations from afar. We can then be more objective and less critical of ourselves.

Life won't always be perfect or the way we would like it to be. There will always be mountains to climb. We just need to keep on trekking. My old college friend and I used to voice the old saying that—"What goes down will always go back up again." We must keep trying, and all things will eventually change. Sometimes the down times last a long time. But remember, if we stick it out, all will get better. We don't want to miss the wonderful events in our future by giving up during the discouraging days.

Our despair might come from divorce, the death of a family member or friend, illness, losing your job, rejection and insults from a friend, bullying, or many reasons far more important than my own, which were my failures at fulfilling my dream.

I know also that little things can depress us. A person can treat us disrespectfully at work or socially, and suddenly we nose dive into sadness. We don't want to dwell on the small injustices. Life can be a wild ride of highs and lows. We shouldn't want to isolate ourselves from people. Don't do like I did and hide in your apartment. Life is too precious. Little things can seem so important, but we must remember how small our failures are in the totality of our lives. When we fight back against our failures, we gain confidence. We are worthy and valuable. We must remember that. We are important to our families and friends, and especially to God.

We must keep respecting ourselves. God thinks we are important, so we must stop putting ourselves down. He never told us that life would be simple. He won't make all our problems disappear, but He is beside us. I like to imagine that He is holding my hand. He is holding yours too. He wants us to keep trying. It's easy to give up and hard to keep going forward. But fight. And don't forget that God loves us, whether we succeed or fail.

As long as we live, we should try to enjoy our journey and be proud that we tried. We can't give up on life. Let's pat ourselves on the back and keep doing so. Have courage. There are so many that stop striving for their dreams, but it's not going to be us. My courage has returned, and I'm back auditioning. You have courage inside you also. Hug yourself.

We are all vulnerable and often become our own worst enemies. But we have good qualities, and lots of them. Write them down every time depression wants to win. I bet you'll be surprised at how many wonderful qualities you have inside you.

Don't give up on going forward. At the end, we'll all be glad that we didn't quit. The good things won't come to us if we don't try. Let's keep up the fight. We *are* worth it. Let's go forward. We can do it!

Chapter 6. Loneliness

We all have times when loneliness brushes over us, and at other times where it overwhelms us with the heavy cloud of sadness. It sticks to us, and we are desperate to shake it off. Sometimes we can't seem to make it stop. We feel completely alone.

The causes can be very real, like a death in the family or despair over illness. In each, we can feel terribly alone. It can also be from the accumulation of rejection and disappointments that hammer us daily. You may feel it's up to you alone to deal with the repercussions and problems, and you might feel embarrassed to say you need support. It's possible you think that no one will care about or understand what you are going through.

Let's think about the disappointments that burden us. We tend to bottle them up inside us and then feel intensely isolated. Maybe you've lost your job. If you were the main bread-winner, you soon realize your family can no longer make the rent or house payment, or even afford food and utilities. Feeling ashamed, you don't tell your family or friends. You isolate yourself with problems big and small. You get discouraged and feel like a black shadow has enveloped you. You don't really want to burden those you love, and want instead to put on a show of strength; yet still the isolation is depressing you.

Truthfully, you need other people. You don't have to bear the weight of these problems or deal with daily struggles alone. We all need to talk to people about what's bothering us.

We all have at times very real reasons to be lonely and depressed. Don't be embarrassed about it. Tell your family. Tell your friends. That's what they're there for! They are supposed to be there for you through your happiness, sadness, fear or despair. If they don't seem to care, they are not true friends, having resigned themselves to the status of acquaintances or work relationships only. On the other hand, even when you need the people who do care about you, you find some of them are vulnerable to overly stressing; they can't handle your burdens and become as troubled as you are.

Nevertheless, families are meant to work together. They need to know how you are feeling. They can't help you if they don't know and you don't ask. So be strong, you can do it. Ask for help.

It is true that some families function more as a unit than others, but you should still try asking. If it doesn't work with your family, there are always professionals that you can seek out. There are psychiatrists, social workers, doctors, and community self-help groups. Many are listed each week in the local newspapers and on the internet. Try joining groups that share your interests; this can bring you more friends and get you involved in interesting activities, where you can share in the experiences and the fun. Group ideas may include bowling, playing cards, astronomy, painting, dancing, theater activities, sewing, and lots of others. Most local communities offer individuals the opportunity of joining low cost activity groups. Check your library and city hall for information on them. There has to be at least one that will be to your liking. These groups are there for you after all; most are on the lookout for new members, would love having you join and will cheerfully welcome you. Don't be afraid to try. If you don't like one, try another and keep going until you find one that fits not only your interest but where you also like the people. Have fun with it.

Again, don't bottle yourself up or hide away in your house or apartment. Go to church or visit a community event, try striking up a conversation! Be brave. There will be people there who like to talk and who would love to converse with you. Of course, if you intuitively feel the person isn't interested or should be avoided, turn away and try talking to someone else. There are all kinds of people in the world, even some you will really like.

You can always compliment someone as a conversation starter, we all like compliments. It will not only make the person feel good, but you as well, and this can often be the start of a friendship. In this way, you will lift the veil of loneliness, that fear and responsibility have caused.

Remember also to seek professional help if your loneliness turns into deep-seated depression. You are who they have been trained to serve. They need you as much as you need them. Without clients, they don't work.

We all have been lonely and depressed, sometimes deeply, at one time or another. We need to make contact with others. It brings us out of the cloud of bearing the burden ourselves. It lifts the emotional weight of struggling through life alone. Don't be embarrassed.

Decide to converse daily. Talk with someone, even if it's only briefly, so your hovering sadness can start to lift. The feeling of being alone in your struggle is only valid if you let it remain so.

There are some people who would rather be alone. Possibly for them, being with people saps their energies, or they simply like the quiet. But many individuals need to talk to and be around others. It invigorates them, bringing joy into their lives.

When I was young, I always found it easier to reach out and socialize. For some people, it's the opposite. Regardless of age, many people feel more alive and confident around others. If that is you, don't let pride or embarrassment keep you from socializing so as to combat the loneliness. We think we don't want to bother people. But most people will not feel that you are a bother, because they also love to talk and socialize. Just speak up. They probably will be flattered and happy that someone wants their attention and friendship. They may need you just as much as you need them.

Don't feel you are the only one that is lonely or that you are too proud to seek people out. Everyone gets lonely at times. You'd be surprised how kind people can be when someone admits that they are feeling lonely. I know initially it will be hard to get started. Try not to be shy. Just jump in.

Loneliness can cause you not to enjoy your life. But you deserve to get the best out of it. You have a right to be happy. You are not a burden. You are welcome to share who you are. There are good people in this world, so trust your feelings when you meet them.

Casual conversation will boost your confidence. Don't give up on making new friends, as well as cultivating the old ones. Maybe they are just as lonely as you but are afraid to act. You never know until you reach out to them.

I think God sends people to intervene sometimes and help us out of our isolation. It can often be a friendly welcoming person who chats with us in a group or talks to us in a store.

A friend of mine had an experience of that type once. She doesn't usually get spiritually personal in our conversations, but one day she did. And her experience got even deeper into kindness.

My friend said to me that while she was in her shop by herself and waiting for a client, she had an emotional experience. She told me that she had been feeling very alone and depressed. Suddenly a woman walked by and knocked at the door. Thinking it was her new client, she opened that door. The woman was not the expected customer. This stranger smiled kindly and said, "God loves you." Then she happily turned away and was soon out of sight. My friend said that she was shocked that this woman had said exactly what she needed to hear. She had been feeling so lost, sad, and alone. She was very moved and now felt so happy. My friend expressed the thought that maybe the lady was an angel sent by God. She asked what I thought. I told her that her story was wonderful and that I believed she was right.

We'll never know for sure if we were both correct. I do know that the woman lifted my friend out of her sadness and loneliness. It also made me feel excited and positive. Perhaps God had sent this stranger to my friend, or maybe she was just a person who likes people and honors God. Either way, the words cleared away my friend's depression, and put in its place happiness and love.

I believe God is watching over us all and may send people into our lives when we most need them. They can be real living people or heaven's emissaries.

God loves you and does not want you to be unhappy from being alone or otherwise. So, let's fix it. Hug yourself and go forward with confidence. You are uniquely and wonderfully made. Give your loneliness the boot!

Chapter 7. Fear of Death

As human beings, we are aware of death. We are stunned when we first see a family member or distant relative in a coffin. It may frighten and confuse us. We don't understand how someone we love can be there in their bodies and then not. The body looks so unreal in death.

When I first saw the casket bearing my twin brother, Tom, I was numb. He was killed in war and blown apart, so the military had shipped him to us in a box and said it should not be opened. I stared at the box. It didn't seem possible that he was dead, let alone in that container. I felt suspended in reality. I also felt terribly alone, lost, and confused. I couldn't believe he was dead. To this day, I still think he lives somewhere. He had red hair and was very tall. Whenever I see a tall man with his hair color, I always stare. My heart skips a beat, and I question, "Is it him? He never truly died to me. He is somewhere, just not with my family or with me.

My father died years later. He too had a closed casket. And again, it felt unreal. He didn't feel gone.

Then many years later, it was my mother's time to go. She was very old. I had fallen asleep and was suddenly awakened by her voice. She called my name—"Linda." I jumped up and hurried to her. Her oxygen machine was still pumping. I thought I must have dreamed her voice. A few minutes later my sister, Diane, came into the room and said that she was dead. I couldn't believe it. She had just called to me. I touched her cheek and was terrified. Why was she so cold? I suddenly realized the truth. Her soul was now gone. I was shaken to my core then, by the reality of death. Did she dissolve into nothingness, leaving just this empty shell behind or was her spirit alive? I quickly concluded that she still lived. She had called to me in my mind. Her voice had not sounded frightened. She is in another place, and it's a *wonderful* place. She always believed in God and heaven, and I think she is very happy in God's house now.

Perhaps we all question whether death is truly the end. Religions console people with various concepts of the afterlife. This does comfort us. I always feel sad for true atheists. How can they bear losing family and even think of dying themselves, when they believe that lives are worthless in the end? As for me, I truly believe, there is life after death and a heaven. It is so because God has promised it.

Also, I have had some visions and spiritual intuitions that reassure me of an afterlife. Of course, one can never know for sure if the things we witness in visions are truth or just our lively imaginations, but I feel all I saw was true. I hope so. I don't see visions often; in fact, they've each occurred many years apart. And I seldom saw them when I was young. Please know, I'm a very practical person, despite my love of the acting profession. I've also been an elementary school teacher for many years and a waitress. Practical and sturdy occupations! I know I'm not crazy. I've worked hard all my life and have been exposed to a lot of different people, lifestyles, ideas, and experiences.

When my uncle was very sick, I was over visiting my sister, Diane, in Illinois. We had planned to drive to Minnesota together to see him. He had been a novelist and short story writer for many years. He later turned to technical writing, so as to better support his family. He was well-read and had a highly intelligent mind. He was also a lively personality. When my brothers and I were children, he used to tip us upside down and show us such wonderful joyful times. I always adored him, even though he didn't support me in my goals.

At the time, I was planning to write and produce my independent films. I guess my uncle figured they were impractical, and I suppose they were, if you wanted a steady income. But I idolized him for his enthusiasm, his mind, his talents, and the way he strove for his dreams. My uncle was my dear father's brother. I wanted him to embrace my going for my goals. My father had? I wanted his encouragement also. I was trying so hard. And it hurt that he didn't agree. You hope that everyone will support you. They may care about you but not voice positivity on your dreams. However, you can still love them.

My father was charming and also had the mind of a genius. He would often sit at his desk in the basement den and have four or five history books open. He would read voraciously. I always felt inferior, although it wasn't because he thought so; my insecurities were all my own.

My father always made me feel special, however. When I was in college, he wrote me many delightful short notes. One, that I especially treasure, said:

> *Dear Linda,*
>
> *I'm watching a movie with Jennifer Jones and Gregory Peck and thinking of you.* (I adored Gregory Peck.) (Then Dad scribbled lines across the page.) *Woof! Duchess* (our dog) *says hello.* (More lines across the page.) *Gregory Peck is now kissing Jennifer Jones.* (More lines.) *Here's a dime for pop.* (The coin was taped to the page. Soda was called pop in the Midwest.) *Mother says hello and come home and visit.*
>
> *Love, Dad*

I loved being in my father's presence. He inspired me. He also dreamed of being a writer and had published some short stories, but family responsibilities kept him grounded and from continuing towards his dreams. Both my father and uncle were exciting to be around. I admired them tremendously.

I don't mean to forget my mother. She worked hard. She also found time to sew me beautiful doll clothes, cover me up with blankets when I slept, and read me fairy tales. When I was a teenager, she would come down late at night and see me either struggling with sewing a garment or typing a school term paper. She would sit down and pitch in as I collapsed on the table with my yawns and snores. I remember those times and smile.

On this day, my sister, Diane, and I decided to visit the graves of our parents and brother Tom. It was the day before we were to leave for our uncle's house. We sat down on a bench there in the cemetery and called our cousin to say that we would be setting out early in the morning.

Gravely our cousin told us that she didn't think her dad would make it until then. This hit us hard. I was feeling very emotional as my sister continued talking on the phone. I had wanted so badly to see him one more time, yet he was going to die that night. My childhood idol would be gone forever. I fought back my tears.

Suddenly I looked up and outward. There in the graveyard I could see our deceased mother, father, and my twin brother walking up to us. The light around them was bright, but our mother was especially radiant. Mother had died the most recent of all, and I thought maybe that was why she looked so young, beautiful, and happy. She had died a few days before her ninetieth birthday. In those later years, she had hated looking older and being physically handicapped. She had breathing problems, needed a walker to get around, and was hunched over with back problems. But here before me was this young, strong, gorgeous woman, her old age and disabilities gone.

They were all smiling. My father was in the middle and my brother beside him wearing his army uniform. My father spoke enthusiastically and said, "Don't worry. We'll be there to meet him." I gasped with wonder and joy and turned to Diane. "Did you see them?" I gushed. They were gone when I turned back. I looked at my sister. "It was Mom, Dad, and Tom." I was awed and very excited. I told her about the vision and Dad's message, she believed me. And that night, my uncle did die.

Was this vision true? I don't know if you believe it, but I do, as does my sister.

I'm no longer afraid of death. I don't want pain, but I think there is more to our soul's future. Freed from the body, souls may hover or leave immediately and possibly return when they feel it will help us. It helped my sister and me that day.

When my younger brother, Gary, died at fifty-eight years old, I missed him terribly. He and I were always close. As children, we made cakes together and ate them until we were sick from the sugar.

My two brothers and I once built a three-level tree house in our apple tree. We each had our own floor, rickety though they were. We argued at times but were always "family." My sister, Diane, was five years older than my twin and me, so she was more fascinated, at that time, with boys her age than us. I would listen to her stories and idolize her. She once showed me a list of all the boys named Bill that she knew and liked. I was awed at how long the list was. I also remember how she babysat us when we were young. She used to do somersaults and tricks to make us laugh. My biggest memory was all of us hiking in woods, ravines, and over the railroad tracks in rugged areas. Those were times when you could be gone for the whole day and parents didn't think anything of it. Maybe they should have worried. Now, I think we were crazy to do that, but we had fun. Happy cherished memories. We were truly family.

When Gary passed away in the hospital, my sister-in-law and I returned to their house and our hearts ached. Suddenly a bookshelf collapsed. The house continued making strange creaking noises and pings for days. We felt it was Gary greeting us, and always we said to the noises, "Hi, Gary!" We were so silly about it, though it spooked us a bit at first. Addressing the incident made us feel better. Many years later, we still thought, however, that it was Gary reminding us that he lived in the afterlife. That's good, because we still missed him.

Gary's house was in Phoenix. After the funeral, his daughter asked me to hang onto my mother's grandfather clock that Gary had loved so much. She had flown in from her home in Hawaii, and the clock was huge. It was also too heavy for her to take back on the plane. My sister-in-law was going back to Hawaii with her daughter, and they were going to clean out the house for selling. In just two days, the house was empty; we loaded the clock into my car, and I drove back to my home in California.

My son was on his own then, so I had no one to help me carry the clock into my house when I arrived. With lots of effort I managed to get it inside, but I couldn't put it up on the wall. I staggered with it and finally hefted it onto my piano bench.

Months later, my girlfriend, asked me to attend a group psychic session with her. We were to meet the famous psychic, Brian Hurst.

I was excited to go, and the night was fascinating. Mr. Hurst went around the group and talked to each of us. I'll never forget what he said to me. He told me that a man keeps urging him to tell me to go home and check the clock. I was confused and didn't know what he was talking about. The meeting ended and that was that, I thought. That night I learned, much to my surprise, why Mr. Hurst had told me those words.

After I had gotten home and flopped onto my couch, I suddenly heard a "gong" sound that kept on repeating over and over. I gasped and raced into my den. I looked at the massive grandfather clock laying across the piano bench, where I had left it all those months ago, and it continued to "gong."

But how could it make these sounds while it lay on the bench? The key had been lost, so I had never wound it. I stared at it in disbelief. I felt a chill and amazement, and I laughed with excitement. "Gary! GARY! YOU'RE HERE. Gary. Thank you. I miss you." Suddenly the clock's "voice" stopped. After a moment, I tentatively moved back into my living room and listened to my now silent house. I started to cry with joy. He was alive. I grinned.

I called my brother's wife and their daughter the next day, and told them the story. They laughed and agreed it was definitely Gary. We spoke of his smile and of our many delightful memories. We also knew that we would see him again someday.

From this and other experiences given to me by my deceased family members, I have come to believe that we don't need to fear death. There is an afterlife. I hope that my experiences reassure you too. Don't be afraid. There is more to our soul's journey, and the dead don't forget the living. They will always love us.

Chapter 8. Good Fortune

Never- Give- Up. Why? Because you never know what good fortune and blessings are waiting for you! If you stop believing that positive things can happen to you, they surely won't. But if you believe, through the good times and bad that all will work out for the best, then in the end, it often does.

Now it's true that accidents, illness, and the sudden death of loved ones can stop you in your tracks and even shake your beliefs. But the pain and loss we experience in our lives comes with having free will, through our environment, and basically living in a world where other people exist. But if you believe in good things happening, they will happen—be it in this life, in Heaven, or in the next life through reincarnation. I think, we can have many lives, if we wish them.

I do believe that blessings can come to us through hard work, positivity, and an openly calmed mind. When I quiet my mind, I'm surprised by the blessings I receive. It doesn't always come in the time frame I want, but it does come.

Keep dreaming and working towards your dreams. Some people say that we should frequently picture our dreams in our minds and see ourselves interacting within those fantasies. This positive energy is a force for accomplishing those goals we dream of achieving. I will admit that sometimes the universe surprises me because it's timing for bringing about these positive things are not always as fast as I wish. But it still happens.

For many years I would occasionally throw away dollars on lottery tickets, hoping to come into some windfall. While it's important to note that good fortune doesn't have to be monetary, I must say I was surprised just a few months ago when, for me, it was just that. It came out of the "blue" so to speak. I got a big check from a class action settlement. Usually if you get anything from a class action suit, it's a check for ten dollars or one for fifty cents. Unexpectedly, I got a large sum, one that amounted to thousands. I asked the bank if it was authentic and if I could really cash it. I was afraid it was a scam. Well, it was real! Good fortune can be a total surprise. Which means there's still a chance I might get my "knight in shining armor" someday. I'll keep thinking positive thoughts.

After all, thinking good thoughts can't hurt. Often it can help a lot. You'll feel better, and miracles still happen, even small protective ones. Hopes can come true, maybe not always but sometimes.

For instance, I was walking my dog some years back. The wind was blowing hard and I shielded my eyes and stepped sideways. I don't know why I did that. It was not the dog pulling me or the wind. But I suddenly looked back and was surprised to see a hole. I was amazed I hadn't stumbled into it and fallen! I hadn't seen the hole even though I had been walking right towards it, and my dog was a frisky pup having too much fun to worry about me. But because I had stepped to the side and turned, I had avoided falling! I gasped and couldn't believe it. What made me do it? Then I knew, it was God's blessing. Now I have fallen in the past, and broke my left shoulder once, so God doesn't always intercede. But I felt like He did this time. I was shocked and emotional from the wonder of this small but significant blessing.

So, good fortune can come when we least expect it. Try your best to stay hopeful. When negativity comes, wave it off and tell it to go away. It's hard sometimes, but worth it. You'll be happier. I think God and the universe He created want to bless us. You are not alone. Keep dreaming and stay positive.

Chapter 9. Dreams for Your Future

Unless you have sincerely lost interested in them, don't give up on your dreams. If you have achieved contentment, your goal may simply be to maintain that happiness throughout your life.

If you have big dreams, however, the pursuit can certainly be exhausting; I know from experience. Also, they can take you away from earning a steady salary or reaching a more socially approved goal. But whatever it is you choose to do, you have to want it. And in order to be driven, you have to want it badly.

Wanting to pursue several dreams at the same time is an acceptable goal. You can get sidetracked, take a detour, and that's fine too. It all depends on your wants and needs.

But I've always clung to the belief that we don't want to die with our dreams still curled up inside us. Dr. Wayne Dyer used to beautifully call our dreams—our "music." It is good to take breaks from your goals to refresh your energy, but remember, the years will go by fast. They seem to pass slowly in our youth, but they do gallop along later in life. If you want to reach your goals, keep trying. People, ill health, financial problems, and aging can try to stop you, but don't get discouraged. If you want something, as long as your efforts aren't hurting others, keep striving for it.

Don't let negative people or circumstances discourage you. I know it's easier said than done, but keep going. The amount of effort you'll need to expend depends on how much you want to succeed. The effort is all up to you. If you lose interest, it's fine. Only quit if that's what YOU want. You can replace your dreams and desires with others. God just wants you to be happy.

I had a dream of writing, directing, producing, and acting in my own full-length independent films. I did so twice. I never made enough money to pay myself back but I was proud that I never gave up.

I had been acting for years, including roles in independent films. I had also produced, directed, and acted on stage a lot. I had played small roles on television. Loving both film and television, I had read every book I could find on filmmaking. I had written lots of short stories, speculative screenplays, and an unsold novel. I felt well-rounded enough to handle my own film company. It was my dream and I was going to do it.

At one point, I remember being very frustrated on how I was going to make the technical part work. I called an audio engineer, listed on the internet, who ended up being a life-long friend. I sat beside him, and we happily worked together. He later introduced me to an editor, who loved the project and became a dear friend as well. It took years to finish that part of my projects and it was hard work. Many times I was intensely discouraged but tried to keep my goal in front of me. I didn't want to fail at my dream. I just couldn't give up, and we finally got the films completed.

I found a low budget distributor for my first film and another for my second one. I was proud of the works. As I said, I never made a lot of money on them, but I achieved that dream. There were many tears and fears and thoughts of giving up, but I couldn't face the prospect of not finishing those movies. Sure, they might have been better if I'd been more well off financially, but then again, maybe not. Either way, my heart was in it.

I did, however, end up refinancing my house a couple of times, so I'm not sure I would recommend my financial choices to others. In fact, you're better off finding other financial means to fund your dreams rather than paying for it like I did, on a teacher's salary and my home equity. But I've never regretted going for my goals. It took me a total of seven years to finish my two full-length films.

I sent my movies to my uncle afterwards. He watched them and never really criticized them. I think he was surprised at my work, or at least I like to think so. We spent a lot of time discussing how he and his daughter disagreed on the meaning of one of the films. He thought it all took place in a dream, while my cousin believed it had been based in reality. Their discussion pleased me. Perhaps he found my work interesting. I like to think I earned his respect. I know my dad would have been proud. He's looking down from heaven, with a smile, maybe. I like to imagine that.

I will admit that all through my struggles, I wrote and directed my projects while on vacations from teaching school. For years, I would edit my films on the weekends. It takes longer to complete a project while having a regular job, but at least you can still eat and pay the bills. But even having my son to care for, we did fine. You can raise kids too. He actually helped on my movies, made lots of friends, got paid, and had fun. We figured out how to make it work within our lives.

You don't have to bury your individuality and dreams under the pressure of family obligations. You can have both. It brought me closer to my son. I think and hope children are inspired when their parents have goals and still want to make them come true. But you must not neglect your responsibility to your family. Let your heart have both. Sit your family down and discuss how you will manage your time, and help them understand that when you are happy, you can't help but be a better parent and spouse. You must pledge to keep the family a successful loving unit. Ask your children and spouse if they have dreams. Tell them you'll support their efforts too. But don't let yourself get overwhelmed by responsibility. Get organized! Ensure that everyone's voice will be heard.

Never forget that your family is there; they will be your support during the ups and downs. It might actually be easier with a family, considering the emotional support they can offer. Either way, with a family, a spouse, or even as an individual, you can still have dreams and pursue them. The endings may not be exactly what you pictured, but at least you went for it. The endings may even be better than you imagined. Plus, you can say you tried. That's so much better than not trying in the first place. Be proud of yourself, and if you fail, still be proud. Everyone who has ever succeeded at anything has also failed. We just need to get back up and keep trying. Don't give up unless you gave it your all and/or are content with moving on.

I think you'll always be glad you tried. Listen to people, hear their advice; if you like it, try it. If it doesn't make sense to you, don't bother with it. It's really up to you. You want to be content and happy in the end. Just remember, it takes work.

Your dreams could be far different than mine. Your dreams may be to get married, to have children, to work for an airline, to serve in the military or in a service area. You may want to open your own business, become a lawyer, or an environmentalist, a teacher, a singer, a writer, an actor, a musician, a doctor, a scientist. You may even want to open your own business. I could go on and on; there are so many wonderful goals in life!

If you find yourself detoured, and you are happy there, then stop. If you are unhappy and wish to continue, keep going. You might fail along the way, but remember most people do. The bigger the dream, the more often you might fail to achieve it, at least at first. I've failed many times at getting acting jobs and selling my screenplays. My movies never became blockbusters, and I cried along the way when I failed too. We are only human.

If you decide to quit, I repeat, be proud that you tried. If you try again years later, that's great! You can keep going, if it's what you want. Only death can stop you. As for failure, it does bring humility and helps you understand and be kinder to others. If it becomes too hard to carry on, be gentle with yourself. Don't hate and torture yourself over it. You can stop; it's really up to you. Everyone fails sometime in their lives, even the rich and famous. Many people win on the second, third, even fourth tries, but seldom on the first. They just keep their dreams alive, revise them from time to time, and even replace them with new ones. As long as you live, you can still dream and try again. Or not. It's your life after all. Live and be happy. God will always love you.

Chapter 10. Following the Winds of Time

Time goes on, both before our birth and after our death. I believe we are pulled on our souls' journeys by special yearnings and needs. It is up to each of us. When we have met our needs or fulfilled our purpose, we may move to another level in God's realm. I believe our journey includes reincarnation, if we wish it.

I do think our sins are forgiven by God if we ask for such blessings. If we have been cruel, I think we can recognize our flawed and harmful behavior and either ask for forgiveness or try to do better and make amends in another life. For those who have no desire to repent and want to live in darkness and unhappiness forever in the afterlife, it is there. We do have freewill for our souls, and actions. In the afterlife, our eyes are opened to see how the way we lived impacted on others.

But living our present life is very important. We must not take it lightly, for living is a gift. We must use it to the best of our ability. We must not intentionally throw it away. God won't hate you if you give up, but you'll only go back to learn the lesson again. I know life can be terribly hard at times, but you are not alone. Don't give up. You don't have to struggle totally on your own.

From people I've met and from my own experiences, I believe there is more to a soul's journey then that which we see now; this comforts me. People may say I'm crazy but what a good way to be if it brings happiness to you, and leads to kindness to and from others.

I remember my first and only regression hypnosis with a guide. I had read a lot about regression and wanted to see if I could better understand life, death, and God's plan for me.

During the session, I was nervous and didn't think I would feel or see anything. I was surprised that I did. Did I just make it all up in my imagination or was it real? I don't know. But I'm content with the good feeling it gave to me.

In my regression, it all had a dreamlike quality, like I was floating with a body that I couldn't feel, while inside my head I still felt like me. One moment I was lying comfortably on my guide's couch. The next minute, I seemed to be sitting in a round outdoor patio with many doors. Suddenly a woman appeared beside me. She had white hair pulled back in a bun. She quietly seemed to welcome me without speaking. I felt safe. She took my hand and then faded and reformed quietly into my father, who had died. I felt no fear. I was so happy to see him. I hugged him, and he felt warm. He told me I was safe and could go through any of the doors to see the past, if I wished. I didn't want to leave him at first but then I choose.

Through a door, I suddenly found I was back in time during the Civil War period. I was a male soldier who had died. I was crumpled up on a field. There was no sound. I could sense my body's bloody brokenness, and yet I felt no pain. I slowly sat up and peered over at the twisted bodies of the other fallen soldiers. Slowly they began to heal and sit up. There was mist all around. A man came towards me, and I saw that it was my brother Tom. He reached out his hand and pulled me up. I felt very light as I rose. I gazed down at my body in fascination; I was a Confederate soldier while Tom was in Union garb. He smiled and led me through the thickening fog now swirling around us.

Suddenly I felt myself forming into an old lady. I looked around but Tom was gone. The air cleared. I sensed that I was sitting in a rocking chair on a porch outside a rustic cabin, in a glen near some beautiful woods. The sun shimmered brightly. I looked down at my hands, now aware of my bony old frame. I felt the urge to reach out, and I grasped at the outstretched hand of an old man in a second rocking chair nearby. I couldn't see his face, but I knew I loved him. I felt immense happiness. Then he faded. I suddenly returned to the present and felt dazed.

My guide asked if I'd like to continue the regression. I said no. I was trembling with an all-encompassing awe at what I'd seen. I was intensely happy. I had seen my father and brother and had felt their love. I had seen my brother and other dead men regain life in another dimension. I was overwhelmed with my emotions, and soon left.

My guide had recorded the session, but I never listened to the tape. I just never want to break the spell of that wondrous feeling I had had. Was it real? I hope so. It also helped me to not fear death. It comforted me, because I had seen both my father and brother who I had missed so much. I sat in my car for about a half hour after the session just enjoying the euphoria.

Maybe my imagination conjured up the whole experience. But, it made me think that life is eternal and that I shouldn't let chunks of bad events discourage me in my life journey. Don't be disheartened by yours either—please. There will be so much more to our life adventures!

Chapter 11. Why Me?

Do you ever ask yourself— "Why me? Why do such difficult and bad things happen to me? Why can't I always experience luck and good stuff instead of the bad? I'm a kind person. Isn't there any justice in the universe, or even in God's plan? Why do bad things happen to good people and good things happen to bad people?"

We don't know all the answers. Only God knows the why? But we can certainly ponder, speculate, and guess.

Those who go through past life regression may theorize as I do here. Some may cry "Nonsense!" and say that life is arbitrary, ending only in death. I don't think so. I like the belief that the difficulties were planned, because God loves us and our souls learn from living. I don't like to look at it as a punishment; I don't think it ever is. It is a learning experience. It may be for others in our life to learn from us, or maybe we are the ones who need to learn. I like to think that we have a choice, be it in this life or a former one. I also think that we can chose to not be born over again, that our souls may stay in the heavenly realm instead. But God made this world for us to live in and experience. We mess it up sometimes but not always. So, let's live in it!

When things go very well in our lives and we are constantly blessed, I like to think we planned the calm and those loving happy periods. When things go badly, I do feel that there is teaching going on and to an extent it was planned that we should learn.

Therefore, whether you agree with me or not as to our soul journeying through various incarnations, I do think that all is not totally random. I think we have doors in our lives where we can continue on our present journeys, or escape and move on to the Godly realm. We can choose to give up, but our souls don't want to. However, God isn't forcing us to stay. We have free will. Ideally, we would want to learn from our experiences or lessons, and to experience living. But if we can't handle it, there is forgiveness. But don't give up intentionally. There is always something good coming too. You will never experience the good if you give up.

Sometimes living can be hard and painful and at other times totally WONDERFUL. If you look back at your life, I'm sure you can remember good moments even in the darkest times. They may be just a simple kindness that was unexpected or a glimpse at the wonders of nature or even love for a child, man or woman. God does not want us to give up. Every day brings possibilities for beautiful things. Life is constantly turning, and can turn around for you. Take a moment and write down the good experiences in your life. It might be laughing with your siblings or parents, the sweet smile of a child or the innocence of a baby, playing as a child or loving as an adult. There must have been small moments that you cherish. Think on someone you have loved. Even if it didn't work out totally the way you wanted it to here on Earth, you have loved someone. Someone did love you. That love was and is precious.

Every day brings new things, new people, and different experiences. The bad will go away. The good will come again. It may not be on our schedule, but it will come. Be patient. The sunlight will shine again, and flowers will bloom even after the darkest storm, new life will come into the world, people will fall in love with people, animals, and activities. New people will come into your life, as well as new events; there will even be some happy ones that you will come to hold dear. The bad will pass away.

Even in sadness, you become moved emotionally and though it hurts, it does lessen. You are left with bittersweet memories. Ultimately, it is better to have good memories of someone even if that person has died, than to never have been a part of his or her life at all. It is better to have felt love at least once, even if that love moved on in the end. Even if you only had one friend in your life, treasure them and the memories.

Because we exercise our freewill, we choose to experience the good and the bad. We choose to feel. We choose to live and die by being human. We choose whether to love or not, embrace others or reject them, to charge forward or run away. But the positive choices do bring happiness.

Don't give up. Life is always moving us along even when we want to stay still. Every day will be different. You'll never live this day again except in memories. But you must go on living if you can. If you give up, you cut off any chance of ever meeting the wonderful people and seeing the lovely events that could happen in your life. True, you won't experience anymore pain on this plane, but if you give up, you'll never know the happiness you left unclaimed. Life brings new feelings every moment. Don't let one or more dark days tell you there is nothing ahead of you, because that is a lie. Your soul will get stronger, especially during the dark times.

Time never stops, though it seems to go slowly when you are young, you'll look back one day when you are older and think time went in a flash. Your older self would say to you: "Don't worry so much. Treasure who you are. You are unique and special. You are a shining light from the divine. You are one of God's children."

You'll look back and be happy that you never gave up. Plus, you don't want to die before you've tried reaching for all your dreams. If the universe brings earthly illness and death sooner than you planned, perhaps it was for a reason that you chose in God's realm. Perhaps your soul will grow stronger from the experience. If you fight to be, do your best, enjoy your life, and be kind to others along their journeys; in this way, you'll die with love and happiness in your heart. And that is a good thing.

Thus, my friend, be patient, keep trying your best, reach out for and to others, and never give up. You are God's wonderful creation, and most assuredly you are loved.

Chapter 12. Roadblocks

We all experience roadblocks. They pull us up short. We can be chugging along happily toward our goals and successes when all at once they rear up in our path like wicked monsters. They can be frightening or just horribly discouraging.

Roadblocks can cause us to feel like we've been suddenly buried and are smothering, or that our feet are now encased in cement and we can't move forward. Often, we cannot even take a step back so as to regroup and start again. Our emotions can be flooded with discouragement and despair.

Perhaps:

> You got fired or laid off in your job.
>
> Your husband or wife left you, or you had a fight and that became a separation.
>
> You or your spouse got seriously ill; even worse, maybe it's your child who has become very sick.
>
> You husband, wife, dear friend, or child has become violent and his or her life is going in a downward spiral.
>
> You are having legal problems.
>
> You feel like nothing good has happened to you in a very long time.
>
> You've worked hard to attain your dreams yet now it seems like you are losing ground.

In each of the above, it can seem like your world is ending and you want to give up. Don't. Tomorrow will be different. It may get worse before it gets better, and that's hard, I know. But that hollow sick feeling in your stomach, that hopelessness, will come to some resolution. The pain will subside. It can seem that life spirals up and down and back and forth; in truth, it isn't a stationary object. The world is always turning on its axis and so goes your life. If a death plunges your family into darkness, you will eventually resurface. Just like being in a swimming pool, you have to surface in order to take your next breath. And you need to breathe to survive. The future will bring good things as well as the not-so-good. You must survive and keep trying or you'll never experience the good things.

Sometimes roadblocks last a long time, even years if you are familiar with the crushing weight of debt. But you will get out. You'll either keep on paying until you get the debt squared away or you can go bankrupt, even the later will not tarnish you forever. To many people, bankruptcy is a solution and a relief, and a way to happily begin again. That's what it is meant for, so you do have a solution when all else fails. You aren't a bad person for doing it. We all need practical solutions to bring about the end of our roadblocks and troubles. We need an ending and a hope, and we must work for the best answer we can find. Sometimes we have to make U-turns and changes but we must go on. Our lives are too precious to not fight for.

Also, we must remember not to judge others along the way. We are all different and have different stress peaks of what we can handle.

One huge roadblock can be experiencing the death of a friend or family member. There is a hole in your soul that feels as though it will never be filled again. You feel raw because your life has experienced a sudden and drastic change.

Please know, God has not deserted you. He is right beside you. Lean on Him. Feel His love. Your terrible emptiness will close over with happy memories of the deceased, if you let them. You will move on in your life and be happy. You will remember those who have departed fondly, but you will still fulfill your own life with many more happy years.

I personally feel we will meet those family members and friends again. In another life or time, the same cord that binds you both now may still exist, just slightly altered. The sex may change or the relationship, but you will feel the same familiarity and warmth, the same attachment and possibly, the same love.

Do you ever feel, now and then, that you've met someone before? You find you feel very comfortable with that person, could you have met him or her in another timeline or life? It is comforting to think that maybe someone who's died in your present lifetime will be tied to your soul's continuing journey, that you will possibly meet him or her again.

I love that part of life. What a wonderful feeling it can bring! I think it's God way of giving meaning and hope in our lives. You may or may not decide to accept the reincarnation theory. The living can never really know for sure. If you prefer to think of just having a wonderful afterlife in heaven, that too is worth living for.

If you don't believe in God or Heaven, then maybe try to accept that time changes people and events. There is happiness as well as sadness in our future and the cycle of life constantly repeats. Try to remember the happy times—I'm sure you have some—for they make life worth living.

When you get to the roadblocks, try to relax and quiet your breathing. If you feel the fear come upon you, push it away or imagine it dissolving and floating off into space. Quiet calmness will help you make better decisions.

You are God's child, His treasure. You will always be forgiven when you make mistakes. Don't dwell on troubles. Don't get stuck in heartache or worry. Kick those roadblocks away and enjoy your life in your own special way.

Chapter 13. Choices

If you are depressed and feeling intensely lonely, don't be afraid to make changes in your life. You always have choices. Many people, having a deep-rooted feeling that things are not going to get better, remain in houses, towns, or jobs even when these things continue to make them feel trapped. This lends to the feeling that they can no longer go further in reaching for their dreams. Please don't do this; this is your life, live to enjoy it and satisfy your soul's needs.

Still, don't aim for excess just for its own sake. You won't be happy with money just for the sake of having it. Money is only worth what it buys, and that should be things that will make your life easier and more pleasant. Its best use is to fulfill some purpose, and move you closer to your goals.

If you don't own your own home or condo but instead rent an apartment because of lack of funds, feel free to strive for more. Because it's your life, you can always make the choice to change it. Material possessions may or may not fill an emptiness in us, but making a change will often bring you closer; it's up to you to try!

Marriage and children may fill a void, and be the change you need and want. Of course, this arrangement isn't for everyone; some people like the ambience, lack of stress and general quiet that comes from living alone. I was a single parent and loved raising my son. Now that he's grown however, I find I also enjoy living on my own because there is now less responsibility and less demand on me. I love my child but I also love my new freedom to pursue my own wants without guilt. I like the change. But single life can also bring loneliness. Everyone is different, and we all have a different balancing act when meeting our needs and achieving fulfillment.

If you want to challenge yourself and go back to school to improve your life, and feel more fulfilled, do it. You'll be surprised how much the schools will try to help you, not to mention your family and even your friends.

There might be other avenues for help with childcare if you have children of your own. You could trade off your days with other parents, or volunteer at a daycare center on certain days during the week so that your child will be taken care of during times when you have classes. Ask for help; if you are willing to seek out aid, you will usually find it. There are amazingly wonderful people in this world who will touch your life, sometimes just when you need it. Remember them when you feel discouraged. And of course, we must remember to pay it forward and help others in return.

I made the decision to go back to school when my son was about four years old. I took out a student loan and was waitressing at the time. I met a wonderful woman in my class who offered to babysit for free during my evening classes. She said that she wanted more companionship for her son and daughter. The woman was kind and giving and the children played happily together. My son thought it was a treat to go there, he loved it. And this meant I was able to finish getting my full California teaching credential, without the stress of paying childcare and worrying about the quality of care. This lady was my human angel. I'll always remember her kindness.

I realize I was given a gift. I had tried many babysitters that my son didn't like. He was shy and quiet as a child but did open up about each sitter when I asked. There was one instance where the child care woman allowed her children to sit on the chairs but not the paying children. In another there was a question of abuse towards a little girl. I removed him from those homes. He only stayed where he felt kindness and love. Always ask your children for details when using sitters. Many are wonderful, a few are not. Children are God's gift to us. Their welfare must always be given prime consideration in our life choices.

If you are miserable or feeling overwhelmed by emptiness in your life choice, then reset your goals, evaluate your hopes and dreams and take a hard look at your environment.

Over the last two years I've taken some months between apartment leases to live in New York. I loved my times there, although I did come back for good and rather discouraged from my job hunting as I said before. But New York was on my Bucket List! I also loved coming back to California. You might be surprised to know I drove both distances, seeing towns both large and small in between. And my wonderful sister, whom I've mentioned before, is also a travel agent and has taken me with her on several trips outside the country. I will admit, it's a fascinating time in my adult life. It can be in yours too. While I now consider myself to be fancy free, I always do check the funds in my bank account. Still gone is the need to plan out my life as I did after college and while raising my child and maintaining our household. There're highs and lows with this way of life but every day is new. You can go forward on different roads in life, you can also make detours or go back if YOU want and are able to do so.

The world is yours. Have wonderful adventures. Meet different people. If you fail at something, try again, or try something else, if that is what YOU wish. All the great scientific and technical achievements in the world involved a history of failure (sometimes up to a thousand failures), but the people who achieved them did not give up. Your failure may be humiliating but you don't have to call it quits. I know very well how hard it is on our egos and sense of self-worth when we fail; I cry sometimes too. It may take many tries and changes, even years before you succeed the way you've always wanted. But we have to pick ourselves back up and keep going, believing for what we want in our lives and making changes as needed. Don't fear change.

Our wants don't have to be aimed towards money aggrandizement. It's not always satisfying just to make money. It's what you do with it that counts. The most fulfilling dreams may come from helping others.

Whatever we choose to do, always remember: try not to bring harm to others. We can affect others greatly, just as they can affect us. As God's children, we must remember to be kind.

Some pitfalls on your road to change may be exposure to toxic people. Be aware that these people can bring you down and make you feel defeated. They can drain you of your energy and positivity. Take advice that seems logical and reject anything that seems motivated by ill-will; it is presented only to hurt you. Some people get satisfaction from putting others down. Often, it's because of failures and short-comings in their own lives. Moreover, there are other kinds of people who will try to discourage you from making changes, because they don't want you to be hurt by failure. They may sincerely care about you, but it is your life not theirs. Just keep in mind when you first reach out for the happiness you want, you might fail. But if you don't at least try, you will definitely *never* succeed.

Watch that you don't pressure yourself too hard or let others do the same. If you feel the pressure exhausting you, maybe you need to pull back for a while or try a different approach. You need only give up if it makes you happy. No one should judge another for doing so. If they do, try to ignore them.

Depending on where it's coming from, these nay-sayers may have a meanness in them and are taking it out on you, or they worry about you experiencing the pains of failure. And yes, failure hurts when it happens, but the hurt subsides. Let the memory of it make you stronger and more determined if you feel you have chosen the right path.

If you make mistakes, accept them. Sometimes you can learn from them. Other times the forces against you are just beyond reason and understanding, but don't forget that there are forces pulling for you too! Even if people don't say so, they do admire those who work for change, striving for betterment or for attainment of goals. So be proud of yourself.

Little changes can help you love your life. Changing jobs if the pressure is too much. Getting a pet if you haven't found someone to love. Changing your housing arrangements or environment if you find it isn't working out. Adjust your lifestyle if you are feeling drained of energy or just don't like the way you are living. Sometimes making sudden changes are good, sometimes not. Weigh your options, be thoughtful in your choices and do your best. That's all we should really want from ourselves: our best efforts. And don't be afraid to change. Find a friend or confidant with whom you can discuss the pros and cons of the changes you want to make so you will feel more prepared.

If you don't like the way you look, you *CAN* change yourself. Ask for help if you need to, but always remember you are a wonderful person. God loves you the way you are, even now, and He will still love you the way you want to be. You are great in His eyes.

You can make changes. You have choices, and you are not alone. People will be there for you, and if they aren't, God is always there and ready to pick up the slack. I believe there are angels beside us too. If you can't solve the problems on your own, turn to others for help, and still try to believe in yourself. You deserve good things. If you want change, go for it. You will be respected for trying and you might achieve what you never thought you could do. Be high on you and all that you can achieve. Don't give up unless you see something better than what your original dreams and goals contained. Love yourself and make changes if you need them. God is beside you! Say to yourself: "Life will not defeat me. I will be happy." Say it over and over again until you can no longer forget how true and sweet it is!

YOU ARE NOT ALONE

Chapter 14. Listen to Your Heart

As the old slogan says, "Stop, Look, and Listen." When we are troubled, we need to stop, calm down, take deep breaths, and listen to our inner voice.

Unfortunately, people can hurt each other terribly; it's a very disturbing fact and the effects can last a lifetime. You may be in a heated or building argument with a friend, co-worker, boyfriend, spouse, or child that's quickly getting out of hand. Stop before you both say words that you'll later regret. Instead, listen to the goodness in your heart. Don't let hateful words escape your mouth when you are angry because, like a weapon, they can hurt—badly.

In the heat of a moment, people can get carried away with cruelty, and their desire to be right can outweigh their reason. Once the fight is over, the awful things said in disagreement are the ones remembered forever. I'm sure we all have heard someone saying mean hurtful words criticizing someone else. Some of us have even heard such words directed at us in the past, and we have never forgotten them. You can be told you are smart or attractive dozens of times, but when somebody says they don't like your appearance, or tells you that you are stupid or incompetent, such words stay in your mind your whole life. Please, just like we do not want to be hurt, let's start by not hurting others. Listen to the kindness in your heart. Listen also for words of helpfulness and answers to our problems.

I still remember being a shy, vulnerable teenager. I'm sure many of us may remember our teen years that way. Personally, I always seemed to struggle with my weight; I thought I was fat. I look back now and wish I was still at that weight. I wasn't fat, just not skinny. Still, around that time, I decided to lay out on the grass in my backyard to try and get a sun tan, thinking it would make me look less fat. When I came back inside, however, my mother told me I shouldn't lay out in my bathing suit like that because both she and my younger brother thought I looked too fat exposed in that manner. They meant well, but this crushed me, and I never laid out again. I struggled with my weight and self-esteem from that moment on. I never thought I could be pretty.

Those simple words from my family have lingered forever in my memory. I can look back at them rationally now and know my self-worth. But still I admire people who are fat or different yet don't let their weight or shape stop them from buying whatever kinds of clothes they want. I still buy blouses and dresses with sleeves because I want to cover my arms, and I still don't wear anything that shows my shape, even though I did get thinner. Words, even said by people who love you and whom you love in return, can hurt. And criticism, even the kind meant to help, can be terribly damaging. We must examine our words and not be careless or thoughtless in the advice we give to others.

I remember losing lots of weight as a waitress. I was happy, thinking I looked fairly good. But a trucker casually yelled out to me one day: "Hey, Linda. You lost weight. Lookin' good, but you still got fat legs." Then he laughed. I was devastated and humiliated by the comment. I knew he liked me and meant well, but it would have been better if he weighed the words in his head and heart before speaking them aloud; I never did forget that incident.

So, please, let us listen to kindness in our hearts before we criticize someone with the aim of helping them. There are other ways to help besides pointing out faults.

After my graduating from college and gaining my California teaching certification, I waitressed and taught school most of my adult life, and still teach as a substitute occasionally. It is from this position that I have seen both adults and children hurting each other. Feelings are routinely getting hurt, with fractures forming in those fragile self-esteems. "She's my friend," cries out one child as she pulls a second child to her. She yells at a third child, "She's not your friend," The third child cries and is very hurt. And there always seems to be a bully, child or adult, who thinks that to strike out and humiliate others is somehow empowering, that it gets them the kind of attention and reputation they want. Wrong. Simple words like, "Fat boy" or "Ugly girl" are overwhelmingly hurtful. Sometimes a youth may have behaved badly, but instead of handling the matter privately, the adult begins shouting where everyone can see, humiliating the child in front of his or her peers. Even if the child deserves punishment, it shouldn't be done with harsh or humiliating words, or physical abuse. Often a firm talking to at home will do.

Adults need to control their immediate disappointment and anger, take their child aside, sit down, and then voice concerns. Ask for an explanation, and then discuss and decide on a punishment, if one is needed. We must all control our anger. Even if we have had a horrible day at work, we must sit down, quiet ourselves, and gain control. We must - *Stop*, *Look* (Think), and *Listen* to our own inner voices of kindness. We need to stop those negative voices of outrage that can pound in our heads when we are upset. We don't ever want to make a person feel that he or she is not loved or respected, because God loves and respects each of us; therefore, we must do the same for one another.

Look and listen also to the beauty and quiet of the universe. We need to clear our heads of our hostility and anger. If you need help, use your imagination to think of quiet things or tranquil places that you like. Think of swimming in cool water on a hot day. Think of taking a warm bath after a hard day of work. Look at the clouds drifting by. Relax… Calm down…

Occasionally I would take my students outside to lie down in the grass and have them tell the person beside them if any special shapes appeared in the clouds. They would say cotton balls, snow balls, snowmen, rabbits, fat snakes, and all sorts of sweet things. We would imagine stories between the cloud shapes. We would then head back inside and write down our "cloudy" tales. We were calm and quiet and happy. Sometimes we would draw the flowers, the trees, the school, or our favorite outdoor activity, or even our own ideas.

We can all go outside when we are upset. Go, lie down in the grass. Let your mind wander. Feel the breeze. Inhale the smell of the plants.

Appreciate the beauty. Draw or daydream a story. You might even write it down into words. Have fun, be kind to yourself, enjoy your universe. Nature is a gift to you. Feel the love in your heart.

The world is not all bad. Some of it is wonderful. We are alive. We have air to breathe, and ground to stand on. We have clothes to wear and often at least one friend beside us. And most of us have a place to call home. So think of good times and feel free to go out and make even more good memories. You deserve the best. If you are missing any of the above, talk to people about it and try your best to find ways to have your needs met.

We want you to enjoy this world. Don't be afraid to do so. Be brave. If the first person that you ask for help rejects you, ask others, and keep on asking until you get the assistance you need. It's your right to have help. "...seek and you will find;" God told us these words, therefore, don't give up the search. Others are seeking the same as you. We can always work together to find the answers.

Listen to your heart and follow your instincts. You deserve happiness and deep down, you know how to find it. Just don't flirt with danger in order to achieve it. Work for your dreams and goals. If you don't try, it's never going to happen. And as for winning the lottery, if you don't end up one of the select few who've actually won the jackpot, that's fine; it might even be a blessing in disguise, considering that most lottery winners lose all that money in a year or two, and end up even more broke and discouraged than they were before. Even now, without bags of money, you can still have a happy home, job, and life... In fact, this way is probably better and more assured.

Failure? Yep. It happens along the way. Be strong and find your courage! Remember Apple founder Steve Jobs; when his company fired him, he rebuilt his life so it was even better than it was before when he thought he'd failed. We can all look back and see hurtful failures, but there were successes there also. Do you have children who grew up to be loving and kind adults? Wow, be proud! Do you have friends? Be happy. Do you have a job and shelter? Be pleased.

You still have a lot. You are alive. Most of us travel many directions in life before we settle into one path with some supporting byways. The older we get, the less we seem to worry about other people's opinions. We only want to be happy and comfortable.

Some people resort to violence for answers, please don't! It usually doesn't solve the problem without bringing lots of pain, hurt, regret, and humiliation. I still remember that a relative hit me once when he was drunk. He had never hit me before nor did after. He was a good guy, but as an adult he liked to drink too much. The alcohol changed his personality. That was when he would say hurtful things.

Violence never solves insecurity problems, and drinking distorts thinking. If you notice your personality changes when you drink, STOP drinking. You don't want to hurt anybody, let alone those you love since they will never be able to forget afterwards.

Violence is shocking. Another relative once spanked me for breaking an object accidentally. I was a shy child who always wanted to please, so I felt terrible after she did this. Maybe, if I broke it intentionally, I could somewhat accept her choice for physical attack. Maybe then I would have felt the violence was justified, but I don't think so. Even though I knew she cared for me, the shock of feeling that I was disrespected and suddenly momentarily unloved always stayed with me.

I do forgive both people. After all, the one relative was raised to discipline as she did. She thought it was right. Children were hit often in those days. Adults didn't always stop and try to understand why a child made a mistake. As for my drinking relative, he was a victim of sickness and addicted to liquor; I usually stayed away from him at those times. I know he also cared for me and did regret hitting me. But I can never forget the hurt I felt. The physical pain is long forgotten, but the disappointment in my heart is hard to dismiss. Violence against others should never be considered as an answer to your problems. Wars, on the other hand, are complicated. We'll leave that for another time.

Just remember to look around you. Listen to your heart. Forgive those who hurt you. We all make mistakes, and we must learn from them. Let's vow to be kind, and be happy. And if you aren't happy, reach out.

You are not alone. Listen for answers in the quiet. You will find them. God is always with you.

Chapter 15. God, Happenstance, or Human Power

Is our life directed by God, Happenstance, or Human Power?

The Universe is the totality of all things that exist; creation; the cosmos itself. It can also be the world of Earth, as the scene of human activity. Finally, it can be a field or sphere of thought or activity, regarded as a distinct comprehensive system.

A god is a supernatural being, an immortal deity perceived as having special powers over the lives and affairs of people and over the course of nature. In monotheistic religions, God is viewed as the creator and ruler of the universe, regarded as eternal, infinite, all-powerful, and all-knowing; a Supreme Being; the Almighty One.

Happenstance is chance, an accidental happening, or fortuity better known as luck.

These definitions were taken from the Webster New World Dictionary, the Third College Edition, copyrighted in 1988 by Simon & Schuster, Inc. (I love old dictionaries!)

So, are our lives driven by the power of God, the universe of chance, or our own free will? Actually, I believe it's all three with ourselves being the main power-driver. We have freedom to decide where we are going and what we want to achieve. Because of this, the activity of other human beings affects us. But, as these things happen, God is watching over us. He observes and can intercede if He thinks it is needed; often He waits for us to ask. He is always there for us, but like a parent, He does let us make our own mistakes so that we can learn to be independent in the world. He sees when evil arises from among his creation, but because we wanted the gift of free will, He does not usually out right interfere. These thoughts are my conclusions, and I have come to them as a result of Biblical readings throughout the course of my life and from my daily life experiences.

Sometimes we wish and hope God would show His power more often against the ravages of nature and the evil that some men and women do. However, I think He wants us to know He is always there and that we'll have peace in His heavenly kingdom. Our souls become stronger with each new life challenge.

I like to think we chose many of our challenges in life, making decisions and choices through our many lifetimes, and now, during our daily activities. If we chose them, I do think we have doorways of escape from our lives. They might occur when we are very sick, in surgery, in an auto accident, or during war. God opens the door for us, if we decided on it and/or need to heal in the heavenly realm. We can then move our consciousness to a higher level of human understanding. Feeling this way, comforts me when I lose a loved one.

A friend of mine, years ago, was in an accident and almost died. After recovering, she remembered having been a soul, floating above her body and peacefully trying to decide if she wanted to go back in or rise to heaven. She chose to continue living and was forever affected by the experience in a good way. She said that she felt more at peace and was contented with her life. She was indeed happier.

I know I am loved, and I believe that the difficulties in this life are transitory, and that I can move on to another level or life when I die. So, there is no need to fear death. It's just another step for my soul and yours, if you chose to believe it. As for our loved ones, we can meet them again at some point in time. We may even see those we don't like again, but perhaps it is because we need to work out those feelings. If we can't work them out, walk away. As I said in a previous chapter, get away from those who are toxic. Eventually, I think that they will stop following us through our spiritual journeys.

God can intercede to remind us that He and His angels are with us. I find I am startled by this knowledge, and overwhelmingly warmed whenever He makes a good change in my life, even seemingly small ones.

Once my father warned me to lock my car doors and keep the windows closed while I was driving. It may seem a small event to someone hearing this, but to me it was memorable and surprising because, once again, God interceded and saved me. I was still a teenager, it was late at night and I had been driving for about a half hour. I hadn't remembered to lock the car door, yet as I pulled up to a stop signal, I heard my father's voice saying: "Lock the door." I did. A second later, a man appeared beside the car and grabbed onto my door handle. He hung on as I quickly sped away but, was forced to let go. I saw his face in the rearview mirror as he stood up, unhurt, and starred after me. I was terrified. Honestly, I think God brought my dad's voice back into my mind at just that moment to protect me from harm. I was trembling with relief.

Small incidents probably happen to us all the time. They are reminders that God is with us. It may not be as dramatic as my car incident, but they are important. It can be just noticing the flowers, the lovely sunset, or the quiet snowfall. Perhaps it's the feeling of joy at seeing a child smile. Possibly it comes when you are with friends and are laughing together. It delightfully comes when someone makes a kind gesture and helps you, especially when you are lost in worried thoughts.

I realize, however, that God has allowed some people to experience terrible horrors and violent individuals. God gave free will to all mankind, to every single human being. I believe it hurts Him terribly when people murder each other and injure the innocent. I do believe those hating and destructive people are made to understand in their afterlives the awful repercussions they left upon other people, how they harmed their souls. I think they must make amends in the afterlife or in their following lives. God has His own way of dealing with these individuals. I don't think the living will totally understand God's ways until they are in heaven. I don't believe people with moral deficiencies will *always* be punished for previous transgressions. I'm sure most of them have, and will use these trials to add to the positives changes their soul is making on Earth or in God's realm. We don't remember decisions we've made in our afterlives, except possibly through regressive therapy, if you believe in it. It's hard to live on this Earth and understand God's wisdom and the reasons for many events, but we must believe that there will be justice in the end, and that He will always love and be near us.

Feel the warm silence of our rooms in the deep night or early dawn. The quiet can warm our souls and make us feel closer to God, the Universe, time itself, and our world. Even though we may be physically alone at the moment, you are not alone at all. Treasure each moment you realize this.

Chapter 16. Is One Life Important?

Yes! Emphatically, one life IS important. All lives are important. But yours, absolutely! Allow me to repeat my favorite phrase: You are a child of God. You are so very important. Don't ever forget that!

We watch the news and see terrible statistics of poverty and crime. It seems that people brush off the individuals behind each number. But each number is a human being with different talents, wants, and needs. Everyone is important. That's why God made each of us different. We all bring different personalities, interests, skills, and backgrounds to the table. Life would be so dull and uninteresting without our differences.

What our society values, what's considered desirable or acceptable, has changed throughout history. Cultural opinions are set by men and women who change their beliefs and codes of conduct as often as they change their clothing styles. Despite what popular culture might emphasize, one's appearance is not as important as the condition of one's soul. As we get older we realize just how true this is.

You are special. You can change your likes, dislikes, hair, clothes, weight, beliefs, and activities; but one thing remains the same—you are uniquely you on the inside. Cherish your individuality. I think God created us all so that we can appreciate and enjoy our differences.

Do you really want to look and have the same talents as everyone else? You might say "yes" now, but as you grow older, I think you'll treasure your individuality more and more. Your special qualities, even if you can't recognize them now, are what make you stand out. God values uniqueness and our world needs it. You can tweak aspects of yourself, if it makes you happy, but try to keep your fascinating individuality intact.

Have you ever seen a film where every woman is blond and slim and men are all muscular and tan? Watching the movie may seem fun at first, but after a while, you get bored with everything being the same. Give me some realism, some story, some character, and more variety with these people I'm watching on the screen. While it is true that society seems to adore its current ideas on beauty, what it seems always to forget is the fact that everything shifts; the times never stop changing. In its failure to acknowledge this, our society causes people to needlessly obsess over beauty to the point of finding no meaning in their lives, or in their individuality. Those under its influence may lose their sense of identity, that feeling of being unique and different which is what makes them special.

Many years ago, thin people were to be pitied because thinness was a sign of being poor. Rounder women were preferred because it meant they had wealth. Large noses too were a sign of strength. But over time, appreciation for certain hair colors and body shapes fluctuates. The need for specific talents changes, or goes out of style completely. So, in the face of all this uncertainty, be true to yourself. Appreciate who you are. Don't depend on other people for your self-worth. Honor yourself; love you and your differences. I know it's hard when there is so much media focused on appearance these days, but that makes staying true to yourself even more important. You are more than your outward appearance. Make sure both your personality and looks are special to you; that in itself is beauty.

As for your individual actions, the door is open. You are a force to be honored and respected because each and every person has the power to change the world. All the great changes in the world were started by individuals whose lives took on new meaning the day they acted on their goals, and began their missions in life. When these missions helped people, they were remembered with honor.

But even if you don't want to make big changes in the world, you can still add to it with your special talents and your love. Hopefully your aims are for the good, because you can affect people and change their lives with the choices you make. You don't realize it, but that old saying is very true: "Each man is a part of the universe." You have interests. You work hard. You show kindness to others. You show joy, which is contagious. You are honest and giving. You may even be responsible for bringing children into the world. You are uniquely you and that is splendid. Without you, there would be a hole in the universe.

Just acknowledging someone, or holding open a door for another person can change the tone of that person's day. Every interaction has a reaction, and whether you are aware of it or not, you have an effect on the people around you—small or great. And even the small interactions can become an image in the memory of that person, or those people, one they may never forget as part of their life stories. You are important, and so are they.

Sometimes we think no one cares. Truthfully there are many people who care. Sometimes it's people you don't expect. You just need to seek them out.

Once when I was still in my twenties, new management came into a restaurant where I worked and I was suddenly "let go." Everyone was fired without warning, and the new manager brought in his family and friends to fill our places. He said our checks would be in the mail. Thus, I went from going in that morning ready to work, to being fired and immediately sent home. Needless to say, I was upset. I was living from day to day on my small coffee shop tips and my salary. My son was still a baby. I needed the daily tips for my child and me. What was I going to do? I went home and couldn't hold back my tears. My neighbor heard me crying. She came over and hugged me, and then gave me a couple of her food stamps. She said I didn't need to pay her back, but I knew she too was having a hard time financially. I didn't really know this woman well, but here she was reaching out to me with kindness. I did pay her back. But I must say, those food stamps kept us from total despair. Also, my baby sitter volunteered to sit for my child while I looked for a job, and defer her pay until later. There are good people in the world. They can touch our lives when we least expect it and overwhelm us with kindness. We need to remember them when we feel discouraged and sad.

Many people think you are important too. Accept their help. Later on, give back and help others. But never give up on understanding how important your life and all lives are. Each life has an effect on others, for bad or for good. Hopefully there are more good than bad.

As you might know, lives can change history. Jesus Christ brought Christianity to the world. Thomas Edison brought the light bulb. Alexander Graham Bell gave us the telephone. And there are many *many* more: Martin Luther King Jr., Mother Theresa, Plato, Albert Einstein, Mahatma Gandhi, George Washington, Abraham Lincoln, George Washington Carver, Anne Frank, and the innumerable other special people throughout human history who contributed to change in the world. We treasure those that made good changes.

But every life is important—whether you affect great historical changes or not. If you live with kindness and respect for others, you are a star in God's eyes. Just enjoy your life, care about others, and make your best efforts. God wants you here or He wouldn't have created you. So live life. Your life is important to all the people you touch, and for the happiness of your soul.

Chapter 17. Believing in Hope

Hope? Should we continue to believe in hope? Is hope possible in this crazy unpredictable and dangerous world?

God sent His son Jesus to forgive our sins and share His promise of hope, love, forgiveness, and the promise of a peaceful, blessed life in the hereafter. Of course, we can choose not to believe, but why would we want to do that? What a horrible way to live if you believe the soul just ends in death. We have been given hope for a reason—so take it. It's glorious to have hope. It gives us a reason to fight and want to live.

With hope, we can also dream and work towards achieving those dreams, with delightful plans for better and more fulfilled lives. Without hopes or dreams, we are but sad human vessels that participate in life's drudgery, trudging through the good and bad with no zest or joy. What a dreary perspective to have! When there is possibility in our hearts, we can change our world for the best and make our lives more comfortable and satisfying. We can experience love and adventures that excite our souls and engage our minds. We can interact with our environments and humanity in thrilling and fulfilling ways.

It's true that life can bring illness and even death to those we love, but we did love and enjoy the company of those people as long as we could. This at least was better than not having them at all.

We must remember that many people in the world have it much worse than even the poorest folks in our wealthiest societies. If you have food and shelter, a measure of health and love, or have loved another human being, then you are blessed. If you lose any of these things and death touches you and yours, having known love to even the smallest degree makes you rich, considering some people never experience love at all. Cherish it and safeguard those memories to nourish you in times of discouragement or loss.

As long as you are alive, you can believe in hope. Life will bring surprises, both good and bad, but don't forget to have hope. Life can turn negative so quickly; don't default to the hopelessness you feel inside. If you do feel the dark emptiness of discouragement and despair taking over, turn away and focus on something beautiful in your home, something loving, like a child or friend, a husband, or even a pet. Refocus your attention on the light from a nearby lamp or the sun outside, don't stare into the light but rather close your eyes and let its warm radiance calm you and clear out the dread and darkness you're feeling. Or—talk to someone, anyone; don't stay bottled up! Force yourself to reach out. You'll be glad you did. Life keeps moving, and so must you. Sometimes you have to make yourself physically get up and force yourself to move. Moving brings back hope, and soon, you're back to living.

Now talk to yourself and God. Be kind to yourself in the process. You are a wonderful and precious soul. Hug yourself. Make yourself smile. Let yourself have a future. It may bring challenges, but you have the power to keep fighting. You are special. You are a child of God. If you don't keep trying, you might miss out on something really good. You don't ever want to reach the end of your life without at least trying to accomplish all your hopes and dreams. Don't waste the precious life you have. The future is always before us. But on those goals you didn't achieve, don't beat yourself up. Your soul is meant to go on, be it in this life or in another. However, treasure that you have the ability to dream and act, and try to have fun!

Even the nearness of death brings hope for a life in the hereafter, when we can meet again with those we have loved. There is always hope for the needs of our soul.

Towards the end of my mother's life, my father had long been deceased. Mother was very sick and bent over. At the age of eighty-nine years old, she had congestive heart problems and struggled to breathe whenever she would over exert herself, but she always kept moving and living.

In the days before her death, Mother was staying at the house of my sister, Diane. My brother, Gary, was visiting and assisting with Mom's care. One day, when they were all sitting at the dinner table, mother looked up and started talking softly towards the end of the table. My sister asked who she was talking to; both she and my brother saw no one. But Mother calmly said she saw our father. She said he was planning to meet her again soon, and would take her home. Father had said he would wait for her, and she was very happy. But she said he was gone now. Mother wasn't sure whether he was coming to get her there, or if she needed to meet him somewhere else. He was coming though, and she was excited.

My sister and brother reassured our mother that father would find her, and not to worry. It was a few days before she died. She knew there was an afterlife with her husband, our father, and she was not frightened. She was on the border between life and death. She was already connected to the hereafter.

My Aunt Jean, when she was dying and gazing out of her window, told the hospice worker and me that there was a man across the street on the corner. She said that he was standing still and smiling in her direction, and she didn't know who he was. We looked out but there was no one there. She suddenly smiled. I don't remember my aunt ever smiling broadly like she did just then. She was beaming with happiness. She said he just told her that he was waiting for her. Several times she would move her lips like she was talking to him. The hospice lady and I watched her with mouths agape in shock. Here was this very intelligent former lawyer and teacher believing in a man who wasn't human. He visited her repeatedly over the following days, and then she died. Who was this mysterious man that we couldn't see? Was he an emissary from heaven? I think that he was, but regardless, my aunt was looking forward to her trip with this gentleman and was delighted that he came.

Whatever your thoughts may be, believe in hope. Hope for more in this life you're living now. Believe in your dreams. Hope for happiness in this life and in the hereafter. Believe in having a wonderful life all your own! And don't give up on your soul's journey. It's going to be good. Just believe in yourself, and in God.

Chapter 18. Choosing Life – When on the Edge

Just when life seems purposeless, one can be forced to choose: give up, or go on? There are times when life will give you a cold hard smack across the face. The question is, do we lay back and suffer until life is over, or do we claw our way up, breathe deeply, and continue living our lives. While we will never truly forget the hard days, it is also true that we will always remember the amazing people that give us courage.

I sit here now, writing as I recuperate from injuries as a result of a fall. Yep, I fell again. That which I dreaded happened again. God saw a reason not to save me this time. But, I think I understand. As a result, I added this final chapter to my book of how my life changed in such a new and meaningful way. I also want to share my account of the living "angel" I met from the experience. Both she and the event heavily impacted my life in a positive way.

Looking back, I realize I had been feeling a hopelessness and lack of energy towards my life. Early one morning I was walking my cute new terrier named Muffin. (My other little dog Heidi is gone now. I do miss her.) Deep in thought, I followed sweet little Muffin down the paths that wound around the various apartment buildings where I live. All at once I tripped! I then felt like I was suddenly flying through the air and couldn't stop. In a flash, I debated: break my nose and teeth or side bones? Which would hurt less? I hoped I'd be fine but feared the worst. I didn't want to fall onto the pavement, so threw myself to the side into the dirt and landed hard. Teeth okay, nose still there, hip and shoulder—oh no! They screamed in my head! Stunned by the fall, I lay there in the semi-light of early morning, and I couldn't move. Muffin trotted happily over to me and licked my face. And I thought, "I love you little girl, but you don't realize that our life as we know it is now over, especially mine."

After about fifteen minutes of lying in a painful heap there in the grass and dirt, I noticed a little girl walking nearby. I called to her, and told her that I had fallen and couldn't get up. The words on those television commercials I'd heard so many times echoed in my mind: "I've fallen and I can't get up!" I had always thought that commercial was sad, and now, here *I* was as well. I said to the child, "Would you bring your father or someone to help me?" She rushed back into her apartment and returned with her older brother and his friend. They tried to help me up, but the pain from being moved was horrible. I kept saying that I needed to get back to my apartment; I foolishly thought I'd be okay if I could just get home. I didn't think to call an ambulance, being unaware of my broken bones at the time. Besides, I didn't even have my cell phone with me. I just wanted to sit in the warm protection of my apartment with my dog.

With a new idea in mind, my helpers went back into their apartment and came out with their grandmother's rolling walker that had a seat built in. Bearing all my weight, the boys lifted me onto the chair, careful to avoid hurting my shoulder and hip. What an accomplishment! They eased me sideways across the seat, and together, pushed me into my apartment, the little girl following along with Muffin who seemed happily unaware of everything I was going through. In fact, she seemed to think it was fun. She does love people.

As the trio left me in my plump easy-chair there in my apartment, I thanked them profusely. They were the first wonderful blessing I would receive in this nightmare experience. I hope someday, I can show my gratitude for their kindness, and perhaps bless them somehow. They were also kind enough to check in on me a half hour later; I was still in my chair and thanked them again.

As I sat, however, I realized that I needed much more help than I'd first thought. I couldn't move and knew I was badly injured. The girl had handed me my phone before she left, and I called first a friend to get my dog; then after he came, I called 911. I couldn't believe that I was calling that number. "Was this really happening to me?" I asked myself. I knew I was alive and should be grateful, but I was hurting so badly.

The medics soon came and whisked me away to the hospital, where I met trial Number Two. I would have to wait on the gurney for eleven hours without any medication to relieve the pain. The day rolled into night, becoming one long, horrible, painful ordeal. The original quote I had gotten from the hospital staff was a fourteen hour wait. Ridiculous, I know, but they said they were just too busy with critical cases to get to me. This meant the paramedics who had come with me, had to stay by my side until the staff could finally see me. Wow. As if these wonderful professionals had nothing else to do!

I lay there on that ambulance gurney for the next nine hours, every minute in terrible pain. The paramedics were very kind, and stuck it out with me through each of those excruciating hours. At long last I got to Station One of the hallway and into a nurse's care. I remained, however, on a gurney and in the hallway. The paramedics were finally able to depart, and took with them my gushing words of gratitude. I waited with the nurse for the next two long hours until the doctor could check me and give me pain medicine. It was now late in the evening, and I felt some pain relief, at last! All that time, my emotions had been all over the place, swinging between pain, desperation, and fear.

The next morning, I went into surgery.

In the days leading up to the incident, I had been feeling a sense of hopelessness and sadness, thinking that my life wasn't going anywhere. I was very depressed, despite my loving dog. I guess a dog doesn't always work to heal discouragement. I just wanted to go to sleep and not wake up—or so I thought. I soon got violently shaken out of that approach to my life. I'll never forget the nightmare I had just before waking up from that surgery and the days that followed.

For what seemed like a very long time, I was floating in a strange twilight world. As I reflect back on the events, I think the nightmare was probably caused by the narcotics the surgeons had given me. Narcotics always affect me badly, thus I normally never take drugs. So there I was floating, and as I did, I got scared. I kept trying to wake up. I could hear the people talking around me but I couldn't stop floating.

I'd see things get very large and then very small, over and over and over again. I wanted to get out of this crazed netherworld. I was trapped. I knew I wasn't in heaven. I was stuck in a drug-induced nightmare! But now I kept saying: "I want to wake up. I want to live!" I said the words repeatedly, getting more and more desperate and feeling terrified. I later learned that they had given me about fourteen doses of narcotics. Maybe that explains a lot.

When I finally woke up, I saw true reality. I didn't feel any better though, as I was still panic-stricken from the fear. A nurse said that I was okay, but I grabbed her hand, blurting: "Are you real? I want to live." She reassured me that I was alive and that she was real. I kept saying, "Please let me hold your hand." I needed to feel real. Suddenly my girlfriend came in and hurried up to my bed. I was so excited. I cried and said, "Oh, Nancy! Are you real? Can I touch your face? Can I touch your hand?" I grabbed at her hand. I was so overwhelmed at being awake and alive. I grabbed at my own face. "Am I real?" I asked through tears of hysteria. Then I gasped with relief and slowly calmed myself down.

There was a brief moment when I remembered, how I had been feeling depressed at home, and had wanted to hide from my life. I flashed on the realization that there was a good possibility that God allowed me to go through this intense experience so that I would appreciate the life He'd given to me. Perhaps He was telling me that my life was not over, that I was indeed going to live, but I needed to not give up. I was so happy! I couldn't stop the tears of joy and relief. I was alive!

After a week, the hospital shipped me by ambulance to a rehabilitation center. It was a long way from my house. It took an hour of travel. Supposedly that was the only location that my insurance could find that had room.

My son came to visit once, but then he caught a cold and I didn't see him for two weeks, namely because he didn't want me to get sick on top of trying to get better. Unfortunately, my friends weren't able to come visit either. It was a long distance for them to drive, and I understood that. Still, I did feel lonely, and my body hurt terribly. I knew that I would get better, but it was certainly difficult for me.

My heart went out to the others there who were recovering like me, and to those of you who have experienced illness and recuperation. Each of us at the rehab center had lost our independence, and that lose can bring intense feelings of fear and loneliness.

The staff worked hard to help the patients, but it was very difficult for all of us. We were cut off from the lives we knew; this meant we were not only in physical pain but also mentally stressed. Every patient reacted in their own way. Some got angry, others cried, several gushed with the need to talk, while others withdrew into themselves in fear. It was like an intense microcosm of the world. We were all trying to cope, heal, and live.

I know I was saved from my fear by my amazing roommate, Robin. She said that I may use her actual name here. I was so blessed to meet this calm, wise, kindly soul in this traumatic time of my life. Watching her quietly deal with her hardships also gave me strength and the will to keep fighting in my life. Maybe her story will help you.

Robin has struggled physically for most of her life. She is a very gifted woman intellectually and intuitively. She was an engineer, mathematician, teacher, and is a mother, having raised several beautiful children. She has also endured many physical problems, including having to have a liver transplant, and living with diabetes for over twenty years. Once she had even gone into a diabetic convulsion that broke about fourteen bones in her body; she went comatose, and wasn't found by her son until the next day. Along with daily blood tests, she has had to live life in and out of a wheelchair. Robin told me that, a short time before I had come to stay at the rehab center, a nurse had left her on her own in the shower while going to attend another woman. Robin slipped in that shower, breaking her foot in three places; she was now trying to recover from that injury. This lovely woman was having to deal with so many physical problems, and yet she was so calm and giving to everyone. I could hardly believe it!

One night a male patient, who had befriended us, was out in the hallway having a loud heated argument with another patient and a nurse, who tried to help. Robin struggled out of bed and into her wheelchair before calmly moving into the hallway towards the men and the nurse. Quietly she told our friend to calm down and come down to our room and talk. He agreed, and the fight ended. The man wheeled his chair into our room, and I could see he was still shaking with anger; Robin continued to calm him down. I was amazed by how she softly, kindly, and firmly handled the whole situation.

After that night, I was the one who needed help. I was very sick and vomiting. I had pushed the nurse's buzzer many times, but no one had come. I needed help desperately. Seeing this, Robin struggled into the hallway with her broken foot, leaned against the wall, and kept calling for a nurse. She did not leave that hallway until a nurse came to me. Her kind gesture will always remain close to my heart. She stood by me even though we had only just become friends. This kindness meant the world to me. I am so very blessed.

Robin is the kind of woman that you could not help but like. She never gives up on living her life, despite how hard it has been. She is looking forward to getting her own apartment once more, when she is released from rehabilitation.

Robin's spirit burns with a brightness that warms every soul she meets. She is a gift to all. She definitely was to me. Why God gave her so many challenges, I don't know and it's heartbreaking to me, but if anyone can handle it, she can. She is close to God and her family, and she doesn't give up.

Interestingly, Robin told me about a past incident that happened to her when she was at a hospital and in crisis. Her blood pressure had fallen fast and she was flatlining. While this was going on, she told me her spirit rose up and that she saw her deceased brother as an angel with tall feathery wings. She was excited to see him and wanted to touch him, but he stopped her. He told her that it was not her time, that she must not touch him, and explained that she needed to go back. She has never forgotten the experience and knows that her brother and heaven await her someday. She does not fear death, and she loves living. I'm sure that God will welcome her into heaven with loving arms when her time comes. He must be very proud of her.

She touched my life and I am thrilled to have known her. I hope her story has touched your life as well. If she never gives up despite all the hardships that she has been through, the same can be true of us.

We are not alone. In addition to God, we have a world full of terrific people who care! We all need to help each other. We are in this world together for a reason. God is with us, and He has populated our world with many courageous, kind, and fascinating people. Let's seek them out, enjoy our lives, and help them to enjoy theirs. We can make it through the rough times. We really can. Let's choose LIFE. Be strong. Be brave. You CAN do it.

Conclusion

At times, we all feel very alone in this world, even when we have the love of a husband, parents, children, animals, and friends. It may not happen often, or it may occur every day. Sometimes hardship seems to assault us with a deep sense of fear, vulnerability, and hopelessness.

I too have felt these overwhelming feelings. I have written this book as a reminder to both of us that we need to remember and appreciate that we are never totally alone. We are never really lost or left out. It may feel that way, but we are coming to the wrong conclusions.

I truly believe that we are an important part of the universe. We are integral to its existence. Without living beings, the universe would have no purpose. Everything in life has a purpose, even if it is only to exist and thrive. Society, historical trends of thinking, and our own insecurities can take away our confidence and make us feel like we don't belong.

We need to stop torturing ourselves with this feeling of isolation, and instead receive the warmth from the truth that we truly do belong.

We are all important to mankind's progress and most of all to God. He loves us. He wants us to be proud of the world He created. He wants us to search for our hopes and dreams, be kind and respectful to each other, and enjoy our lives. He has promised us an afterlife. I believe we each have a choice between continuing our soul's journey towards improvement and happiness in other lifetimes, or staying in His heavenly realm.

My life has included spiritual visions and intuitions that have affected my life and made me believe that there is a loving God that is always beside us.

It is my hope that you continue on your life's path with pride in yourself, having decided always to keep trying for your hopes, dreams, and a happier life. Please don't give up.

You are special and important. Live your life with enthusiasm and confidence. You deserve a good life. You are loved by the Almighty God and so are never alone. Have a terrific journey, my friend. God bless you!

About the Author

Author, Linda LS Larson, was raised in Rock Island, Illinois. She lived most of her adult life in California and has a terrific grown son, Timothy, of whom she is very proud. She graduated from the University of Illinois with a Bachelor of Science Degree in Education and completed two years of post-graduate studies at California State University in Northridge.

Linda has worked many years as an elementary school teacher, waitress, and actress. She has acted on stage and in films, and in small roles on television. She has written, produced, directed, and acted in two of her own full-length independent films (What Ever Happened to Alice and A Cabin in Time) and three short films. She has in the past written speculative short stories and screenplays, and the novel, Acceleration which will soon be published.

Linda presently resides in Palmdale, California.

YOU ARE NOT ALONE: Don't Give Up is her first published book. She hopes that it helps and encourages others on their life journeys.

For more information, visit her website at:

www.Linda-LS-Larson.com

Other Books by the Author

—COMING SOON—

Acceleration - An action adventure novel.

Love Never Dies: You Are Not Alone – Part 2

www.ingramcontent.com/pod-product-compliance
Lightning Source LLC
Chambersburg PA
CBHW060952040426
42445CB00011B/1112